SEA OF THE
UNKNOWN

Jay Swanson

JAY SWANSON

SEA OF THE UNKNOWN

MISHAPS AND MONSTERS
ON MY JOURNEY TO PARIS

First Issue Edition - 2020
This book was produced with the help of 307 Kickstarter backers

Edited by Richard Bilkey
Line Edits by Richard Shealy
Cover by Kaarin Howard - www.studiokaarin.com
Photography by Janelle Sweeney - @myparisportraits
All of the terrible sketches and cartoons are by Jay

Published internationally by Bad Gustave, Paris, France
This second print run by Lightning Source

ISBN 978-0-9969021-5-1

www.jayswanson.me

For my Dad—Thanks for always being there to listen.

Forward

Once upon a time, in a distant land not so far from here but unpleasant enough that I wish it were, there was a boy.

Contents

SETTING OUT TO SEA

You stand on the Shores of the Known. Behind you rises the dust of a well-travelled continent, the main trail rolling on behind you before winding and branching off into the hills and plains beyond. There's a breeze rolling off the land at your back, warm and dry. The maps available for this continent are decent; the more desirable destinations are well marked and their routes notched with clear landmarks. They aren't free of risk or challenge, but the biggest of the dragons here have all been slain, the ancient places staked out, sterilized, and incorporated into the new. From what you can tell, none of them have what you're really looking for.

Before you, lapping at your feet and crashing against nearby piers, lies the Sea of the Unknown.

It's slate-gray. Cold. While the waves aren't so big here near the beach, there's a lot of chop in the distance. Far beyond the churn and the spray loom the stable specters of your desire. A solitary mountain caught in the sea haze, a lower ridge some miles

to its south. Are they separate islands? Perhaps they're connected by a land bridge you can't see from here. And twinkling just over the horizon like some forgotten star on the verge of vanishing into itself stands what must be a massive lighthouse, monstrous enough to cut through the haze and keep its head above the curvature of the Earth.

Above the chaos and through untold distance, that light calls to you. It's not articulated in the air, but it resonates in your heart as clearly as if you could hear it singing. You've heard the legends; you know others have made it out there, so you know it's possible. Though whether they carved their own path or won life's lottery and hitched a ride on someone else's yacht, the water leaves no trails, and no retroactive map can get you there. There's little sense in standing on this beach, staring at the chaos of the sea with the comforts of known territory well within reach behind you. But the calling never leaves you, not once it's made its mark. Even if there's no way of knowing how you'll get there, or what will stand in your way, you can't let it affect you or you will never even try.

You wander the trail, saving what you can to build your first attempt at a raft. The panels are cracked and the rope is frayed, but you lash one together and push off into the water. It doesn't take long to realize you'll need more than a paddle. As the ropes dissolve and you fall into the sea, you're simultaneously ashamed and relieved to see how close to shore you still are. You pick yourself up, your raft a loss, and march back to the trail to prepare your next effort.

This time, you pick up some work that's even less aligned with your future. The people with whom you walk the trail scoff at your designs for a sail made from sheets, your idea to use a sink as your anchor. But deep down, you know it will work this time.

You pull together a larger raft, with space for more water and food. You slather it with tar this time, sealing the water out

and protecting the thicker rope you managed to buy off a friend. The farewells are bittersweet, many marred by comments asking if you wouldn't be better off sticking to the trail. It's the lack of belief that cuts you deepest, but if you won't believe in yourself at this point, then you fear no one will. You put your head down and shove your raft out to sea, not bothering to look back for fear of what you'll see in the faces you're putting behind you.

This time, your raft cuts through the small waves battering the coast. Your sail picks up a gust, and you feel your heart lighten for the first time in as long as you can remember. The sail pulls you faster than you could paddle, your tiny rudder wobbling but holding true. You catch a fish, frying it on a small stove you scrounged from an acquaintance and saving your dry stores for the journey ahead. You don't know if any of the islands along the way will be able to resupply you, and deceptively, they seem to remain stagnant in the distance even as you gain on them. You tighten your belt; you ration and mind your heading. But the wind starts to rise, and the waves along with it.

Clouds roll in, obscuring the sun and your destination at once. You hear the nagging warnings of the voices you left behind on the trail, eating at your confidence as the wind turns to a gale. Perhaps you really were the fool. Invisible rain rakes your face as you pull out your paddle and fight to keep going. You ride high on one wave only to be smashed by the next. Your small mast snaps; the sail tears and flies off into the wind. The rudder no longer wobbles so much as lurches free and skims along the surface; soon, you're paddling just to keep from spinning out of control. Your water supplies slosh free and you can feel cracks popping open beneath you, even if you can't hear them over the roar of the wind.

By the time the storm abates and the skies clear, you're exhausted, bruised, and sodden. You can't rest long, you tell yourself, and you sit up to take stock of your situation. Your mast

is a splintered stub, your water supplies lost or mixed with saltwater. The distant peaks look even farther away than they did when you set out. Were you an idiot to believe so fully in yourself? You know you can do this. At least you thought you could. . . and then you turn and your heart falters as you realize the storm has blown you back to shore.

You still have your paddle, and your raft held together this time. You try to take some consolation in those facts, but you know now it's not enough. The voyage at hand has only become more daunting; in spite of what progress you may have made, you're no closer than when you began. What might be worse, you realize as you drag your shattered vessel back on land, isn't even starting from scratch but crawling back onto the trail long enough to get started again. Listening to the people around you question your motives, your desires, and what feels like your very identity. You stand on the beach for a long time, holding back the tears that threaten to flow.

Breaking now is not an option. Nor will it ever be, you tell yourself. You drop the paddle in the sand and rally what little strength you have left. Whether you ever even made it that far from shore or you were just playing sailor, you'll never know. Dwelling on it won't help. So, you wring out your clothes, and you make your way back onto the trail to try again.

CHAPTER ONE:

KNOWING YOU'RE MEANT TO GO

ATTEMPT NUMBER ONE ~ NICE, 2008

I've always wanted to make movies. It's something that's been core to who I am since I made *Jason and the Argonauts* in the fourth grade. We filmed all over my neighborhood on my buddy's VHS camcorder and I edited on the fly, sprinting home after every take to check it on my VCR. If it was no good, I'd rewind to the previous cut to reshoot—if it was a keeper, I'd try my best to stop the tape at the right spot to cut to the next scene. It proved to be much better cardio than my workflow as an adult.

I didn't own my own camera until after college, but I was fortunate to have a school system that purchased such frivolities and made them available to students. Every project that could be a video was a video. I steadily dropped out of sports in high school and spent more and more time sitting at a computer like the isolated nerd I was destined to become. Storytelling, while naturally a social art form, requires an ungodly amount of alone time to develop before the social parts can happen (unless you want those social parts to be awkward).

These dreams would stick with me all the way to film school and beyond, after I quit film school because I realized that I hated film school. My French minor became a French major, I kept making short videos and skits, and then I wound up in France.

I've always wanted to live in France. I don't really know why, but there was a magnetic pull from the home of the baguette. My loyalty to the idea came early, formed out of the ether of Madeline cartoons and posters of the Eiffel Tower in my geography classes. It was embarrassingly strong. In my middle school, Spanish classes were available starting in seventh grade (roughly at age twelve). French wasn't available until high school, two years later, which I found an utter betrayal of what should have been clear priorities

for my education. So, when they rolled out an experimental Spanish introduction during the sacred space of my sixth-grade art class, I was livid. Not only were they coming for me a year early, forcing me to recite such useful words as *el toro* and *rojo*, but they were doing so by violating the holy pact of ART CLASS. The one place where I wasn't only *allowed* to draw but drawing was *the whole point*. I specifically made my perspective study, a sketch of King Tut's golden casket, look as perturbed as my eleven-year-old skills enabled. He probably looked more constipated than consternated, but that was an honest-enough resemblance of how forced Spanish made me feel.

Of course, as an adult, I regret not taking the chance to learn both Spanish and French; it took a couple of decades for my ambitions to overcome my pettiness. Regardless of the fact that I only needed two years of foreign language to graduate from high school, I immediately dove in and studied French for all four. Not realizing the power of the accent until this point (or perhaps only developing a susceptibility to it around this time), I fell in love with the woman who narrated *Le Petit Prince* and subsequently with the idea of life wherever it was she lived. Unfortunately for our very one-sided romance, I couldn't find my way to France. My parents couldn't afford to ship me off to study abroad, either, and when in college I did manage to swing a fluke trip to Europe, I was stuck firmly in Italy, with no chance to sneak north across the border. So, right after college, I threw caution to the wind and moved to Nice.

I chose Nice for a few reasons. One was that it had close ties to my university program, so nearly everyone I knew that had done study abroad of some sort had done it on the Côte d'Azur. The second was that my church at the time had equally close ties to an organization in the region, and as someone who had never lived abroad before, I found that all of these pre-ordained connections made for an appealing first landing pad.

Unfortunately, this was how I found out that I didn't want to live in France. I'd been far too general in projecting my desires. I slowly came to realize that I had made a mistake—and it wasn't just because of how boring I found teaching English in a French technical school.

Don't get me wrong; I loved my time in Nice. I attained fluency in the language, I made a swathe of new international friends, and I developed a completely different sense of scale for what was "walkable." Nice also taught me how to identify an entire spectrum of urine-related scents I'd never known existed, and it presented me with my first encounters with the mafia, after a couple of cars got torched in front of my apartment one night. All in all, I left Nice thinking perhaps I'd gotten my wires crossed. I really wanted to be making movies, didn't I? Why was I wandering France's most uncomfortable beach? In winter?

(Of course, the one benefit to hanging out on the beach at Nice in winter is the distinct lack of tanning lotion smeared across the rocks underfoot. Not reason enough to go, but the silver lining of a gray stone coastline.)

During this year of solidifying my French and questioning my sense of judgment, I sat down and made my first attempt at writing the prequel to my first trilogy. It was a doomed piece of fiction titled *The Rise of the Shadow King*, and I discovered firsthand just how hard it is to sit down and hammer out a finished novel of any length (or passing quality). Though the experience would be invaluable as I tackled different stories later on, at the time, I considered it a failure and I decided I needed some help. It wasn't a pleasant discovery, failing to finish my first book, but I knew I could get back to it. I thought perhaps I should go back to the States and continue my education. I still wanted to live abroad, and I thought that France was still the place to do it, but I was quickly discovering how limited my visa options were. So, I applied for a

master's program in theology.

"Wait, what?" the knowledgeable reader has just stopped to ask in bewilderment. "How on earth is a theology degree going to help you get back into a country that prides itself on its secularism?"

For starters, I never claimed to be the brightest of children. To defend my nonsensical thought process, in my mind, theology was directly tied to two men who are counted among the founding parents of science fiction and fantasy: C.S. Lewis and J.R.R. Tolkien. They were intellectual giants, professors, and theologians of their own sort. So, why wouldn't I want to follow in their footsteps?

Not only did I need to start going by J.A. Swanson, but it seemed quite possible that without a higher degree in something even more esoteric than a Romance language, I was probably doomed from the start.

I think it's also easy to discount just how perilously lost one can feel at the end of a prescribed course of actions and life choices. I grew up in a university town. College was king. Something like 96% of my graduating class went to college, the majority right there in Pullman, Washington. Everything was clear up to the point of graduation—and the value of the degree itself was incredibly overinflated. "Just get a degree; the jobs will follow" was high among the mantras of my teachers.

But once you graduated? Things weren't so clear from that point. So, why not go back to school and give myself a little more time to figure it out? When you set out to sea a little prematurely, the harbor behind you looks better than it ever did before.

My parents made the trip over as my time teaching English in Nice came to its close. It was exciting to have them there, to share my little life in the south of France as it came to a close. Neither of them had ever been to Europe before, which made our time exploring even more special to all of us. We wandered

Nice for a week before heading to Paris, and my life abruptly and irreparably shifted.

This was where I was supposed to be. *This* was the city I'd been dreaming of. The textured beige of Parisian limestone carved into winding lanes branching off of Haussmannian boulevards capped with beautiful blues and blacks that still serve as the only example of uniform urban construction I've ever found appealing. The monuments, street-corner cafes, and broad walkable stretches made their lasting impression. This was an inspired city—a city where my imagination ran wild.

After exploring Paris for a feverish week, bike tour and all, a resolution took root: I had to make it back. It was May 2008 and the world was full of promise. I didn't know how I was going to do it, but I was going to live in Paris.

BACK IN THE WHIRLPOOL

I wasn't sure how to get back to Paris. I also realized that taking on more debt for a master's was looking like a worse decision every day, especially without any real plan of applying it to a career. I'd already done that once and it wasn't panning out well. So, I dropped out and contented myself working at my alma mater until I could figure things out. The idea of international living had burrowed under my skin since I first read *Tintin and the Secret of the Unicorn* (or insert any of the other dozens of Tintin books I read as a kid), but now it had taken hold in my heart.

Fulfillment of that desire would have to go on an unfortunate hiatus. I was being groomed to take over my boss's position running the university's computer labs. It was a job with which, if we're being honest, I was woefully mismatched. But it

was safe. If my plans of becoming an international man of mystery were hazy and dangerous, working in computer labs with college students sounded like the perfect counterbalance of potential outcomes. In the meantime, while my boss worked up to moving on, I had a pretty sweet gig developing training materials for the staff and upgrading the interior design of the largest lab. To be honest, I was tempted to settle in for a while. Academia was cushy and familiar; it reminded me of home.

Fast-forward to that moment where the state realized they were financially boned.

To say that the onset of the 2008 recession was cruel to me seems relatively fair in retrospect. It certainly felt like it at the time. There are many who took heavier hits, but I think I land pretty firmly in the "I got screwed" section at the middle of the bell curve.

Not only did my boss decide to stay in his position, as it was looking risky to move out, but my contract wasn't renewed, due to a massive hiring freeze, and I found myself jobless in an economy that suddenly had very little use for me. Doubly so in a community that didn't particularly value aspiring storytellers/nerds-of-many-varieties even when times were good, let alone when facing the nation's biggest financial crisis since the Great Depression. I suddenly found myself in a very precarious situation—one that would become a very common story across the country—I had a lot of debt and no real job prospects with a degree that left few clamoring for my résumé (I'm not going to advise you not to get a French degree, but I certainly won't push you towards it, either).

Over the next two years, I would work tirelessly to start freelancing in web and graphic design, dallying in video when the opportunities arose. I struggled. I dreamed of getting back to Paris. I craved the freedom of being my own boss. This was the period of time where I invested a lot of energy into skits on YouTube,

betting on that one viral video that would surely catapult me to fame and fortune. I spent zero energy on my fiction, because the slow grind of publishing a book was mysterious, out of my hands, and seemingly a longer road to making movies, if that really was where I was trying to go.

I finally got a job in a marketing company that didn't want to hire me for my video skills but decided they'd have me on as a web designer. They talked a big game about getting lots of interesting clients on board, shoe brands and car manufacturers, but in reality, they had created a lead-generation front for the payday loan company across the street. I felt as gross to discover that as I imagine you did reading it. If you don't know what a payday loan is, first: consider yourself lucky. Second: it's basically a very high-interest, short-term loan handed out to people in desperate situations and intended to trap them in a cycle of debt they can never escape. It really is that bleak.

Despite allowing me to build up a small amount of savings, the red flags were quickly piling up, and I tendered my resignation shortly after my boss got into a fistfight with his brother in the hallway outside my office. They were raided by the IRS and shut down a few months later.

The little savings I had built up didn't last long. I had an accident on a jet ski early in the summer, which left me with a massive bruise on my stomach that quickly hardened deep under the skin. This required an MRI which, in the end, simply told me that I was fine. The medical costs cleaned me out. The one time I get on a jet ski as an adult. . .

Looking for something, anything, I took a job for the summer enumerating for the census bureau leading up to the 2010 census. To begin with, my territory was the immediate urban area of Spokane, but they eventually moved me north to a broader rural region. I had to drive my 1990 maroon Honda Accord into all

kinds of places, and I only received occasional threats of bodily harm from farmers along the way.

It wasn't so bad at first, but I was soon being asked to trek to the tapered ends of some very remote logging roads. My brief career as an enumerator ended when I drove into a mud puddle that I couldn't drive back out of. I was on a mountain, just below the snow line. It was the middle of summer.

I took off my shoes, jumped out into the knee-high water, and tried to push my car out from behind. Alone. It wasn't a great plan, but there weren't a lot of bystanders on top of the mountain in question. I gave up when I walked back to the window to discover that not only had the car not budged but it spent all that time filling up with water instead, only deepening the quagmire.

There was also no cell service that far out, but I was lucky to get picked up a few miles down the road by a forest service contractor who flew off the handle when he found out what the "gubment" had made me do to fulfill my duties. "They just reintroduced wolves to the forest near here last year! They can't make you do this!"

What little savings I had accrued during this passing tenure as a government agent was quickly absorbed by my mechanic, who had to replace a computer in the floorboards of my mud-logged Honda.

During all of this, I continued making sketch-comedy videos for YouTube, still hoping that somehow it would morph into something financially viable. Needless to say, it did not (some of the skits were almost funny, at least).

Through all of this, I managed to pick up the occasional web design or video client. Most of them paid me eventually, but rarely without a struggle and occasionally with direct verbal abuse. One insult-hound douchemonger threatened to sue me when I finally quit working for him, which turned into a quick education on contract law.

A cool breeze of employment luck came when I managed to score another temporary position as a photo editor for a school photography company. I'll be honest: it was mundane work, but it was also the first healthy work environment I'd stumbled into in what felt like forever. Dorian Photography—you did right by me. Thanks for the lack of fistfights, Mick and John. There's something to be said as well for having a job with very clear goals and boundaries—showing up to get X number of tasks done before clocking out for the day. It left me with a little brain power left over at the end of the day if I wanted to write or try and grow my own projects.

I refocused on building my own business, and the struggle seemed insurmountable. I was losing hope in the future and slowly, steadily, belief in myself. I felt like I had been someone else living abroad, like I had grown muscles that were now slowly atrophying. I struggled to make ends meet—spent many a night staring at the ceiling, wondering how badly the overdraft fees were going to hurt when my loan payment or car insurance premium came through the next day. I moved into a new house with some friends, which provided an upper bunk to stare at instead of a ceiling, but the thoughts and worries were much the same.

At least this time, I was acting as my own crisis burning through what would have been my savings. I kept trying to find work, cold-called businesses with crappy websites to ask if they'd like a less crappy website, did whatever I could to drum up some business. I was not very successful. Wait, scratch that. I felt like a downright failure. I also felt betrayed, like a future that had been promised me all my life had turned to smoke right as I reached out to grab it.

Things got dark. I didn't fully realize it, but I was losing trust in many if not all of the institutions I had trusted since childhood (namely the university and the church). I wasn't just struggling to put food on the table, which I was; my identity was in crisis.

THE
AMERICAN
DREAM

YOU CAN ALWAYS FALL FARTHER

I'll forever remember the day my roommates told me of their daring plan to get into a local pharmaceutical company by picking up temp work and, eventually, getting hired on as full-time employees. It sounded like an ill-conceived script for a low-budget heist movie. It felt like an absolute affront.

It meant going for a job I absolutely did not want that I knew would only detract from my ability to build something on my own. But you can't eat dreams. Sounds like something my grandpa would have said.

And the people around me were quick to remind me that I didn't deserve to attain them, in the same strange tone that was supposed to comfort the saved who truly deserved hell. I'm not kidding. "At least you have _____ [job]. You know that in the grand scheme of things you don't deserve anything, so be grateful." I had a few of these conversations—low-level gaslighting that leaves you thinking perhaps you are an overprivileged piece of garbage for thinking that maybe, just maybe, all that talk about doing something you loved meant you had a chance to do something you loved. Some obscure myth that I heard once or twice along the way. . . the American. . . Pie? American Cream? Something like that.

So, when my roommates told me they were going to try for these temp jobs at a pharma company, the remnants of my soul recoiled. But I didn't have much to do that day and there was a severe amount of guilt involved in staying home to rest instead of work, so I joined them for the interview and aptitude testing. I figured, why not? "If you get some work," my inner optimist chimed in, "you can quit as soon as another design job comes through."

We took our tests (which, if you're looking for the world's most depressing ego-boost, try taking aptitude tests in a temp-

agency testing center) and were assured that getting hired on would be easy enough with the next wave. As a first, intermediate gig, we moved old broken furniture out of a department store downtown.

"This isn't so bad," my inner optimist continued to chirp. "You need the money and hey, by the time you're done with this department store, I bet you get another design client. Outta here before you ever set foot in that place."

When we got news that we were getting hired on at the pharmaceutical company, I was the opposite of excited. My inner optimist lost some traction as I had no excuse not to take the job, no other immediate options, and I was raised to work. My own sense of personal value was locked into this idea of productivity. Of knuckling down and "manning up." I took the gig.

The first real blow was in taking the job at all. I knew it was what I had to do, but I had spent well over a year trying to build something of my own and consistently stumbling along the way— for some reason, this move above all the others felt like admitting defeat. It tasted like failure, and this was before my palate had grown accustomed.

The second blow was discovering my two roommates would be working together, but on a different shift and in a different department from me. I went into this stupid thing with the consolation that at least I'd be hanging out with them doing it. Instead, I was in it alone.

The third came from showing up and donning all of the sterile gear. Getting through the paperwork and being shown to the quality-control line I was supposed to work for that day. Being shoved into a room I knew nothing about and then berated for not knowing anything. Frustrated, they sat me in the corner with a four-inch binder filled to bursting with standard operating procedures.

"Read this; you need to know it." Hundreds of pages that might as well have been written in Chinese. Later that year,

they would spend some two million dollars rewriting that very book so that it would be legible for the established staff, let alone newcomers like me. But in that moment, I sat alone, in the corner cubicle of an over-lit white room, staring at pages that made no sense to me despite four years of higher education. I stared at them, blindly turning the pages out of the simple fear of losing a job I didn't want in the first place, and broke into tears.

GET ME OUT OF HERE ~ PHARMALAND, 2010

The pharmaceutical company in question was housed in a campus of blocky white buildings. Sanitized, industrial, and hierarchical in every way from security access to the layout of the parking lot. The distance I had to walk after parking my car reminded me daily how far down that hierarchy I was.

I showed up every morning, by myself, with a conflicted sense of dread. I was grateful to have work but I hated the job. Taking a job for the money because your dreams aren't panning out so well leaves you with a strange tension, to say the least. Especially when it's barely enough money to begin with. You know you should be happy that you can pay your bills, but also know you're treading water at best. It can't last.

Covering yourself in oversized industry-standard garments doesn't do wonders for the old ego either. I was a nameless, faceless, whitewashed cog in a machine making someone else rich. Stupid rich. Off the suffering of others, no less. While my roommates at least had the novelty of picking venom sacs out of dead yellow jackets (picking bee butts, as they called it) to balance out the mundane nature of their work, all I did was package vials into small boxes and place those small boxes into bigger boxes before sealing them all together and moving them into cold storage, a big cold box. I was so glad I'd gotten a bachelor's degree for this.

Quality control was the other half of the job. Imagine, if you will, sitting on a stool for thirty minutes, squinting through a magnifying lens the size of your face. On the other side of the lens, an endless string of tiny glass vials slides spinning past, filled with what might as well be milk. In reality, it's the time you'll never get back. You're looking for cracks in the glass to show themselves under the light, for anything that doesn't look like milk to reveal itself spinning in the milk (it was swine flu vaccine but I couldn't even find it in me to care).

You spot an irregularity in a vial, you pluck it from the line with your tweezers and place it in the appropriate bin. The good vials get spat onto a metal table where they slide to the other half of the team, who scoop them up with special forks, place them into perfectly sized boxes, and then place them in the appropriate larger box. After thirty minutes, you switch from inspecting to boxing. If you get into it, there are moments where it can be fun to compete to pack the most tiny boxes. There can be something strangely satisfying in the rhythmic pattern of it all. If you have some cool coworkers, which thankfully I had a couple, you might even laugh once in a while and have a half-decent break.

I still felt like I was drowning. Things slowly got better than they were on day one—I got into the job and managed just fine. I even developed a minor crush on one of the scientists supervising us but was too embarrassed by my situation to do anything about it. As I recall, she was my age and really clever. I also recall that I was cloaked in a frock that removed all signs of personality, so whether or not she could tell that I was locked away in there somewhere, under layers of linen and self-doubt, it's hard to say.

Even as a few new clients came through for my smorgasbord design business, the reality came home that it wasn't enough. I couldn't rely on it. I settled into the fact that I was there for the full length of the project—if I could just make it to April, I

would be able to save some money and complete the task at hand. What threw a wrench in the gears, simultaneously boosting and weakening my resolve, was the day my dad told me that he and my mom were considering joining Mercy Ships.

For those of you just meeting my happy little family, there are four of us—Mom, Dad, Sister, and Me. I grew up in Pullman, a small university town surrounded by wheat fields in the southeastern corner of Washington State. For you foreigners (I'm looking at you, French Laura), we're not talking about the capital of the United States here—Washington State is on the opposite side of the country, in the northwest. It's home to Seattle (*Gray's Anatomy*, *Fifty Shades*, Starbucks, Amazon), and is just a hop north of California (California).

For the entirety of my life up to this point, my dad had been a pastor of a small church comprised mostly of college students.

"Aha!" you just shouted, and threw your book across the room. "That explains _____!"

We can get into the nuances of my Pastor's Kid psychoses another time. For now, all that's really important to know is that I was born in Pullman and three years later, we moved into the house that I would grow up in. This is the house my parents lived in up to this point, and my dad was still pastoring the church he'd pastored for twenty-seven years.

This stable track record suggested a solid sense of inertia that I never questioned. My mom, in particular, seemed bent on staying put forever, so it came as a shock to hear him say they were thinking of moving on. Not only that, they were thinking of moving to Africa? On a hospital ship?! As far as midlife crises go, this one seemed to me to be particularly severe. The shock came not so much from the idea itself but that my mom was OK with it. Not only OK with it, she seemed to be all for it.

"You aren't a doctor." I think it was supposed to be a question but I bet it came out flat. We were eating Chinese food from the Safeway deli, down the street from my bunkbed in Spokane.

"No, but they have lots of other jobs on the ship." My dad was a bit reluctant at the beginning of the conversation, excited for the possibilities but I think a little worried his kids wouldn't approve. "They need staff trainers, audiovisual people; they even need a videographer."

Videographer? I'll be honest: I was skeptical. Not because I wouldn't be excited to see my parents off on an adventure, but because I couldn't recall my dad ever shooting any video over the course of my entire life. I asked my sister: she can't either. Simultaneously, a series of dormant synapses sparked to life at the mention of the word.

"The main concern is whether or not they'll let us go to the ship long-term because of your mom's illness." My mom had been diagnosed with early-onset Parkinson's just two years prior. "But otherwise, we're all in."

The conversation stuck with me, not least of all because someone needed a videographer in West Africa. I could do that. They spoke French in a lot of West Africa. I could do that, too.

Images of an ocean, simultaneously real and figurative, began to stir in my dormant imagination. My dad sent my sister and me an email with a link to the website, and I found myself completely enraptured by the idea of this hospital ship. I dug deep into their website, fascinated by the work and this big white ship that worked nonstop to alleviate the suffering of what they called "the forgotten poor." What they did was incredible (and I am not exaggerating, even now—do a search on Google for *Mercy Ships 60 Minutes video* and you'll be blown away). Life-changing surgery for people who could never afford it in countries that couldn't provide it.

They removed massive tumors that grew to the size of the heads to which they were attached: they straightened legs and released burn contractures. They removed cataracts by the thousands. There was no need to sell me on anything—their work sold itself. And they had an urgent need for a videographer. I sent them an email without hesitation.

CHAPTER TWO:
JOINING MERCY SHIPS

SCREENING DAY ~ MARCH, 2011

I could feel the roar of the crowd in my chest. Thousands of people pushed into each other, slowly crushing the life out of a man immediately beneath me. A small girl scrambled frantically to pull herself up onto her mother's shoulders, fighting for air against much-larger bodies. Desperate to keep from being pulled under. Screaming through tears. I remember seeing her out of the mass before me and specifically uttering a prayer for her, to keep her safe.

Sierra Leone's national stadium stood dispassionately to my left, reflecting back the cries and shouts hurled over the tall outer wall that separated potential patients from waiting medical staff. The National Stadium is a standard athletic field, with a soccer pitch in the center of an ovular running track, all encircled by two tiers of bleachers. At a capacity of 45,000, it isn't massive for a national stadium, but it's plenty big. Some thirty meters beyond the base of the bleachers, the outer wall enclosed the whole complex. The "car-gates" at the north and the south ends of that wall were blocked off. Our team had entered through the northern one before sunrise to set up. The main pedestrian gate, or "man-gate," was on the western side, and it was through there that we had planned to admit our patients.

But no one had predicted the sheer number of people who would turn up, and it was very quickly apparent that the preparations were inadequate. I was standing on top of the man-gate, watching in mounting horror as the chaos unfolded below.

Yellow-vested volunteers on the security team swam against the current and to the side, aiming for the relative safety of that main wall and a small gate farther up through which they could be extracted.

When we tried to warn the remaining security volunteers in the crowd below to get moving, it was so loud I couldn't hear myself shout. What had previously been a series of orderly lines to get into the stadium for medical triage now resembled little more than a surging mob. Police officers from a variety of departments strolled along the banks, exacerbating the situation with harsh words and sudden spurts of violence. Recoiling, those near the perimeter pressed farther inward. Desperation for help drove the rest. The pressure on the gate below me grew steadily, and then surged sharply, all at once.

Someone shouted that the police were going to open the gate, which would have been a bad idea if they'd ever had the chance. Suddenly, the crowd that had been pressed into one another found release as the broad doors were ground out of their slots and flung open. Those who had found themselves the battering ram were immediately thrown to the ground, discarded and trampled. The rows immediately behind them didn't fare much better. They were carried off their feet; many of them hadn't touched the ground for some time already.

The wave crashed forward and spilled out thirty feet beyond the barriers. And it didn't stop coming. Some fell as they stumbled, unable to rise again as they were stepped on, trampled, and covered by the next unfortunate soul to fall. They fought for air, to push their way out, and were met with more weight on their backs. Less air for their lungs.

In the investigation that followed, we learned that among the many factors leading to this catastrophe, there were agitators in the crowd. Young men whose medical needs were practically nonexistent in comparison to the majority, but who saw this as an opportunity to cause trouble. Some of those men came bursting through the gate at a sprint, arms in the air like they'd just finished a race.

Hundreds of people poured through the gates at much slower rates, stumbling and fighting not to get sucked into the pile of bodies growing immediately in front of the doors. There was a smaller gate in the ring wall itself that had been slammed shut just before the man-gate broke loose. I jumped down to that inner level—now below the roof of the gate but still above the chaos. It looked like the pile of bodies would never stop growing. On both sides of the broken gate, people were beginning to climb over the wall.

SYSTEM OVERLOAD ~ SETTING THE STAGE FOR FREETOWN, 2011

I'd lived overseas before arriving in Freetown. I pulled a summer in Italy and Germany for my first round, which gave me a head start on the awkwardness of discovering that one's identity doesn't fully transfer from any given frame of reference to the next. My second round was in Nice, France, where I first saw kids burn cars, mobsters burn restaurants, and pimps burn bridges with transactional passion (I witnessed more than one midnight asswhooping on the promenade—cowboy-stroll away). Still, nothing prepared me for setting foot in Freetown, Sierra Leone.

For starters, days in a port near the equator are hot, humid, and short. The sun sets far too early for my tastes when you get close to Earth's midriff. More impressive than this was the sheer volume of people crammed into a very, very tight space. When we arrived, we were given population statistics that essentially were "This city developed to support up to 500,000 inhabitants. Current estimates put the actual population at around 1.6 million." It was cramped.

Living in the port put us squarely in the middle of this. If you've ever been to an event in a stadium, you've probably found yourself trying to leave with a few hundred strangers all shuffling

slowly through the same narrow hallway for a short, miserable moment. Now imagine this crowded moment stretching for a kilometer, with half-meter-wide gutters on either side (filled with something you don't want to touch), in the blazing sun. Feeling squished? Add bumper-to-bumper traffic. Then add motorcycle taxis weaving through the gaps. And then of course the vendors with their goods spread on the ground in front of buildings and shops lining your path.

Don't let all of those original pedestrians disappear from your imagination, and that gives you a pretty solid idea of what awaited us every time we wanted to leave the port for lunch.

Crown Xpress, my favorite pizza place in town, was only one kilometer out. It was a simple restaurant with hard chairs and an austere modernity, and one of the few places I liked that wasn't way out of range for lunch. The choice was pretty straightforward: walk forty-five minutes and get all sweaty (and sweated on) along the way, or drive forty-five minutes in an air-conditioned vehicle and pay for gas. Either way, it was slow moving. Preferences varied, but we walked a lot more than I'd wager you're currently guessing. And yes, forty-five minutes to walk one kilometer.

Just a side note, but one of their pizzas came with corn on it. My friends Cyle and Alex loved that pizza in particular, and this is how I know that both of them are psychopaths who cannot be trusted around small animals or explosives.

As we usually had the entire evening to ourselves, there were a lot more options on the table for dinner. But considering it could take us a couple of hours just to get out of the center of town, it was customary to eat something before leaving for dinner. The stop-go nature of driving in Freetown was mostly a lot of stop, a little go. We would cheer whenever we hit third gear. It put traffic jams into a completely different context for the rest of my life.

Every outing in town for the first few weeks was a blur. It's what being a toddler must feel like, your brain finally able to take in entire environments but without any of the methods for tuning out the noise. The fatigue at the end of every day mirrored my first immersion in a foreign language. I mostly followed friends who had been in western Africa longer, and tried to learn as much as my tunnel vision allowed.

The Sierra Leoneans we worked with and met in the city were kind and hardworking. From that standpoint, I couldn't have picked a better port of entry into my West African experience. But living in Freetown felt like sitting on a powder keg.

The civil war was a vibrant and bloody memory for many. Those who couldn't return home after the war for a variety of acts committed in the field found themselves with nowhere to turn but the capital, which became increasingly overpopulated. Ultimately, this meant that many found themselves living with neighbors who had been mortal enemies only years prior.

All of this was present, and I was already struggling to process it all, when our screening day fell into chaos and ratcheted everything to eleven.

EVERYBODY OUT ~ SIAKA STEVENS STADIUM MARCH, 2011

Let's take a step back to the very, very early beginning of the day. I'm talking four AM early. I had two jobs for screening day: driving and playing music. I was slotted to make two runs from the ship to the stadium, two Land Rover–loads of volunteers. From there, I was supposed to spend the day on the music team.

Screening days with Mercy Ships used to work like a massive multi-stage triage. Thousands of people line up at a stadium or health complex large enough to accommodate. They're screened at

multiple stages along the way by increasingly knowledgeable team members, turned away for any illnesses we don't treat (anything that doesn't fit within the surgical specialties available on the schedule), or permitted through to see the next person in the process.

As they pass through the initial screenings, they eventually get seen by a surgeon or specialist, and then registered to come to the ship for further tests before getting into an operating room. If the surgeon for a given specialty is available, they'll often schedule them on the spot. Dr. Gary Parker, a maxillofacial surgeon and living legend of the organization, is the classic example. He would spend the entire day assessing patients and scheduling them for surgery alongside his team. Compassionate. Tireless.

Something I didn't realize until years into working with Mercy Ships was just how many screenings any individual patient might have to go through before surgery. It isn't just whether we can help them or not, but whether they have any other illnesses or conditions that might render the operation unhelpful or harmful (autoimmune diseases, for example). A lot of these issues only revealed themselves through lab tests, and often at the last minute. There are a lot of patients who were turned away even on the day of their surgery for secondary reasons, which is heartbreaking in its own right.

Screening days like this also served to rally the crew and give everyone a sense that they had a hand in the main mission of the organization. It provided the starting point of many patient stories we would follow through photos and video, and served as a major photo op for fundraising, as the shocking level of need manifested visually in one place. It served a lot of purposes, but, as Freetown revealed, it simply wasn't safe.

Academy students from the ship played and drew pictures with kids in the middle stages of the line. A prayer station was set up for anyone who needed it. I was stationed at the tail end

with the music team to provide moral support for anyone who was turned away by the medical staff.

I wasn't thrilled to be tucked away at the tail end of the experience, nervous as I was in the midst of such a big day. If the stadium was a clock, then the entrance was at roughly 2:30, and I had been squirreled away down closer to 6:00. I remember feeling conflicted, knowing I would have to spend the day trying to console people who had been turned away from what might be their only hope of care. The inequality of the situation was jarring; I certainly didn't feel qualified to handle it from any angle.

When things at the gate began to deteriorate, someone asked for some of the musicians to come forward and play for the crowd, hoping that some singing and dancing could break the tension. Having not yet seen the man-gate, I imagined the gentle incline of a parking garage, a broad, flat surface that would be filled with people who were growing impatient, slightly restless, and who might enjoy a little singing.

We realized the request for music was absurd the minute we arrived. The crowd was already so loud, we could barely hear our own instruments. The press was so intense, we could barely fit through the door to get outside and play. The only people even aware that there was any music to be heard were the ones who could see us directly, so less than a fraction of a percent of the crowd.

I ran to grab a chair for the djembe player, and by the time I returned, the musicians had already been forced back inside. The second absurd musical request was made that we try to play on the roof of the gate.

"They can't hear us," I protested.

"Perhaps just seeing you will be calming" was the response. I can't remember specifically who told us this, but I do remember feeling simultaneously frustrated by the stupidity of it and relieved

that I wasn't getting sent back out into the crowd itself. That's how I ended up with my vantage from the top of the gatehouse.

The initial lines formed for incoming patients had already dissolved into a surging mass. People shoved each other as much to remain standing as they did to move forward. Children clambered onto their parents' shoulders. Heat grew between pressed bodies under the rising sun; thirst spread as water couldn't. The tension rose to a breaking point before erupting through the doors beneath me.

I'll never forget the stark terror of watching that pile of bodies grow as high as the people standing beside it. Shouting for one of my friends to get back before he got sucked in too. I still don't know who exactly managed to get the gate shut again, but it was a Herculean effort. Imagine pulling dozens of people out of a massive pile while simultaneously trying to keep thousands from pushing into the same space. Building enough of a buffer between those groups to swing two massive doors shut again and chain them together.

As I recall from the report that came later (I asked for a copy and unfortunately never got one), it only took a few minutes to accomplish. Standing there watching, helpless, it seemed like at least an hour. I spent those minutes shouting. Shouting instructions at friends to keep them from danger. Shouting at people climbing the walls to get back down. Just shouting.

Time compressed and stretched all at once. There's a clarity to immediate danger, to the sudden rush of a mob. The world stands out in sharp relief while blurring at the same time. Actions happen more than they are done.

As soon as the gates were shut, there were a handful of things that needed doing at once. We still had thousands of people standing out in the sun beyond the man gate, all hope of regaining control lost on that front. There were people trying to scale the

walls from without. Within the man-gate, and before the final door leading into the stadium where triage was under way, there were now hundreds of people who needed to be arranged into a new line before we could proceed. But most pressing were the thirteen people still unconscious on the ground before the gate. Including the little girl I had seen earlier, scrambling to stay above the press. My prayers proved useless.

I ran down and put my first aid and basic safety training to use, teaming up with whoever was nearest to carry one and then two unconscious bodies to the next level and prop them up on their sides in a safe position. The ground around them was carpeted in sandals, bright, colorful, and tragic. Many of their owners had spent what little they had to travel to Freetown and see us. Not only were they likely to be turned away because of the unfolding situation, but many would now return barefoot.

After placing the second person into the safe position, head propped up under one bent arm, knees bent to keep them from rolling on their back, I looked around. I don't know what preconceived notions of medical personnel you have in your mind, but they aren't all built or trained the same. I was stunned to see how few of our nurses were fully functioning at first.

This was a verifiable catastrophe on the day, but many of the volunteers around me showed as deep of signs of shock as anyone who had burst through the gate. I couldn't blame them—I was totally out of my depth as well.

Two of my friends, Dan and Peter, a former Special Forces medic and a firefighter respectively, were not lost in the chaos. They jumped into action, directing the efforts of nurses whose principal training revolved around much saner conditions. They quickly pulled me out of my own haze.

With the gate closed, the patients stabilized, and the immediate crowd-control issues sorted, those of us who had been

in the mix took a much-needed break to eat something. We were all of us in shock, confused, sad, and angry. Many of the unnecessary personnel had already been evacuated. An internal debate sparked over whether to call the whole thing off. What good would we be able to do if we couldn't control the crowd first? The need for safety butted heads squarely with the mission, and the call came down to evacuate everyone except security staff and Dr. Gary's team.

They said I had to leave. I grabbed a reflective vest and told them I was on security.

IF YOU STAY

There's something to be said for shock rendering a person useless—if you get hit in the face with something unforeseen, literal or metaphorical, odds are good you'll be unable to do anything until you've had a moment to process and adjust. My initial shock came when I set foot in the crowd outside the gate at Sierra Leone's national stadium carrying nothing more than a guitar. I could feel the danger like a hot fog.

As I rushed back to the music station in search of a chair, I had my first precious chance to process what I had just seen— not entirely, but enough for my brain to shift back into gear. As the adrenaline altered course within me (I don't know how else to describe the pulsing, ongoing rush of adrenaline that carries you for hours in a crisis), the first emotion to surface from the shock was anger.

How had they let things get this out of hand? Screening days were supposed to be one of the most special occasions during a field service—the day we gathered potential patients from around the country to find those we would be able to heal. The kids from the ship's academy were there to play with children waiting in line,

many of whom would become our patients. There were stations for arts and crafts, another set up for prayer, and obviously one for music. This was supposed to be a peaceful, bittersweet day filled with promise. Today was supposed to be defined by hope.

It was too late now; the chaos was only mounting. But that walk helped a little. Getting a break to sit and eat away from the crowd put me in the right frame of mind to put my emotions aside and act. When the call came down to leave, I chose to stay. It didn't even really seem like a choice at that point—I had to do whatever I could to help.

I wasn't in charge of anything, but a number of things needed to happen all at once, so I stuck close to the leadership team and became a runner. The first thing was evacuating what had been deemed nonessential personnel. Thankfully, the ship's kids, teachers, and a number of others had already gone on the first round of Land Rovers.

There were Land Rover Defenders on site that were ready to roll but whose keys had not been turned in by their drivers (among whom I was one), so my first task was hunting down keys. That quickly transitioned into getting reluctant nurses loaded and on the road.

Once the Defenders were loaded up, there were conflicting directives. Safety was paramount, but in direct competition was the desire to help as many people as possible. Honestly, I was siding much more heavily with safety at the time. I hadn't even been able to imagine what the crowd at the gate would look like—there was no comprehending the rest.

The few remaining medical staff were placed at a gate on the opposite side of the stadium from the crowd, our eventual point of exit. It was there that they would receive what patients we could select and send to them, do a very basic assessment, and then schedule them to be seen again at the ship.

There were some two dozen of us remaining on site, most of whom revolved in support of the medical crew at the exit. My buddy Sam and I stuck with the two remaining executives who hung with the crowd. Fearless. Very suddenly, I found myself one of only four volunteers in the midst of a crowd of over 1,000 people.

I was not fearless. My main desire was to get the heck out of there. I was overwhelmed. The people who had broken through the gate were allowed into the section just outside the stadium itself, where they were guided up an external set of stairs and seated in the shade beneath the risers. Even then, there were hundreds lined up on the tarmac of the curved parking lot before us.

They wanted to screen as many people as possible before we left and, with the help of freshly arrived riot police, got to work. This seemed insane to me in the moment as I looked down the line. It snaked away and off to my right before curling straight back to my left and rising up two flights of stairs to curve along the center of the stadium itself.

In the absence of most of the multiple teams who would normally run the selection process, it was now being carried out by one woman alone. She was a former Marine officer, cool and commanding, but it was still painfully slow. More and more eyes locked on me and Sam. The line edged forward, melding, cutting. Small shouting matches were quelled by riot police, but our armored helpers steadily spread out. The line bent closer to us, and closer still until suddenly it dissolved. Seeing this, those on the stairs surged down, breaking the gate on the landing by sheer volume. A crowd surrounded us, bearing their literal wounds and begging for attention.

Until this point in my life, I doubt I'd seen anything worse than a bloody scalp in person. That one guy who volunteered to get tased in college comes to mind. What I was now surrounded by was beyond anything I thought possible.

One woman unwrapped her scarf to reveal a tumor growing from her neck that reached the end of her shoulder, the skin split open by deeply infected sores. Another showed me the burns covering her arms. They had healed together, fusing forearm to bicep and tricep to chest, locking it permanently against her side, her wrist unable to move from her collar. Dozens of people struggled to move into my direct line of sight, to capture my attention for just a moment. Hoping perhaps above all that I would tell them, "Yes, we can help with that."

I can't remember everything I saw. I only remember doing my best to identify the things I knew we worked with. It's amazing how suddenly a memorized list of diseases vacates your brain when staring straight at the maladies in question. I remember rejecting the urge to recoil—doing the best I could to lean in, to show that I cared. Touching arms and faces of people who might not have been touched by another human being in years. Perhaps decades. I felt helpless knowing how little I could do for any of them.

I wanted to help, but I also wanted to run. Ever self-aware, I rebuked myself for being so selfish (then doubled down by rebuking myself for rebuking myself for wanting to be safe).

Desperation marked the tone of the people at the stadium that day. They weren't violent, even if some were agitators. We managed to screen dozens more people. Even when we finally made the call to leave and sneaked off to the exit, we were surprised by the riot police, who managed to screen their own batch of twenty potential patients. Even more impressive was that they did a good job in making their selection.

When we piled into the final remaining Land Rovers and rolled out of the stadium, we shared a tense calm. Some joked to break the tension; some just stared off into the distance. It didn't take long for us all to fall silent. I'd never felt more in mortal danger, but I'd also never seen so clearly and acted with such certainty.

Despite the trauma with which I would wrestle for years as a result of that day, what haunted me most was the sense of injustice in the entire exercise. What made me any different from the people in that crowd?

Why did that crisis ever happen in the first place? Not why that day, but why in the cosmic sense.

The why of the crisis on the day was something tangible, something with many different, measurable contributing elements. Mercy Ships doesn't do big screenings like that anymore. The transition was slow but steady. We held another screening in Freetown a few weeks later under much stricter security parameters. The next year, we would have a similar-sized screening day in Lomé, Togo, but they began sending the screening teams upcountry to find people near their homes rather than make them travel. That lesson was hard-learned but resulted in good changes.

As for the cosmic why, why people born in one part of the planet should be subjected to abject suffering that no longer exists in another, I still struggle with that one. It's a reality that follows us across the globe, the inequalities that put some of us in beds at night while others sleep on the street. The contrast is sometimes subtle, and other times staggering, but it's universal and, if we aren't careful, can threaten our ability to empathize at all.

CHAPTER THREE:

CANARIES TO PARIS
[A ROAD PAVED WITH
LOVE AND SPLINTERS]

ROLLING BUNKS

I learned a lot during my time with Mercy Ships: how to ride a motorcycle in sand, how to suture a wound (you don't want me doing your stitches unless I'm your last option), and how to pick locks, to name a few. But one of the great loves I discovered was sleeping at sea.

The transition from land to sea is an awkward one, but I don't think I've ever seen a movie properly represent what it's like to set foot on land for the first time in two weeks. I mean, Jack Sparrow just waltzed onto that dock like he'd never even left it. At least he showed the same level of wobble regardless of the surface upon which he sauntered.

Granted, I never had a soundtrack, but my experience was different on a number of fronts. Everyone talks about getting your sea legs but no one talks about needing to find your land-sense-of-god-damned-balance after strolling down the gangway. It's disconcerting to find that the earth is moving with the vigor of the sea you thought you left behind.

Out at sea, I slept like a baby. Everyone gets seasick at one point or another, but thankfully, in the voyages I undertook, I never experienced it. What I did experience was the mind-numbing exhaustion of keeping my balance all the time.

Imagine walking down a long, featureless, and windowless hallway. There are no visual cues or signs of movement except that as you walk forward, gravity's pull consistently shifts from somewhere off to your left to somewhere on your right before swinging back again. This does a number on your monkey brain, which can't quite figure out why everything looks stable but feels all rumbly and tumbly.

There are two sources of extra calorie-burn going on here as well: ONE—walking like a saddle-sore cowboy stumbling home

after an all-night bender in his first brush with civilization after a three-month cattle rush requires extra effort. Spurs or no. TWO— the brain is energy-hungry enough as it is without the whole world tumbling around all the live-long day. Struggling to maintain balance in an ever-changing environment, decoding never-ending optical illusions, and constant motion requires more than sitting in a nice static coffee shop writing at a stable table (hello!).

This means that when it comes time to hit the sack, your gray matter is more than ready to shut down as quickly as possible so it can regroup and try to figure out what the hell is going on. Combine this with the natural bob and sway of the ship, and you literally get rocked to sleep. One trick that helps with this is to find a foam wedge and shove it under the side of your mattress that isn't against a wall. This will tilt you towards said wall enough to keep you from rolling out of bed. Do this and you're set for the best sleep of your life.

Sleeping with bunkmates, however, can be a totally different story. I had one who snored so loudly, he woke the women sleeping on the other side of the steel bulkhead. By vibrating their bed frames. He did this consistently and introduced me to my first real bout with sleep deprivation, which, by extension, introduced me to my first brush with murderous thoughts.

I had another bunkmate who I always tried to beat to bed because his body odor was so oppressive, it felt like a physical cloud (think Pig-Pen from *Peanuts* but without the cartoon charm). If I didn't fall asleep before he rocked up, there was a good chance I wouldn't be able to for hours.

Even then I wasn't safe. I woke up choking on his stink cloud more than once (and I really wish this were a hyperbolic retelling). Of all the adjustments to ship life, sharing a cabin with three other grown men was one of the biggest. But life in Western Africa was definitely full of much bigger surprises.

FROM THE CANARIES WITH LOVE

The Canary Islands. Assuming you don't get swept away by hordes of drunken Englishmen, it's hard not to have a good time. Although to be fair, I'd argue you haven't been to the Canaries unless you've fallen in love in the Canaries. Which means I've barely been to the Canaries, but I've been nonetheless.

I tried falling in love in the Canaries on three separate occasions and failed twice, although I feel like the attempts were worth the failing.

ATTEMPT NUMBER ONE: EURO CUP FINAL WIN

You know those days where you keep crossing paths with the same beautiful person and you start to wonder, is this the real life? Is this just fantasy? Caught in a landsliiiiiiiiiiide, no escape from sorry, sorry. But you know that feeling. This instance involved a Swedish woman with whom I first crossed paths at Burger King in Tenerife. Not the most romantic start but hey, it's where we were. I need to take a moment to thank the ship's head chef for this because he had worked pretty hard over the span of our voyage up from Lomé, Togo, to convince me that a Whopper was actually a decent burger.

I took up his challenge on the day of the Euro Cup final and made my way into town ahead of my friends, who were fine living the Whopper-free lifestyle they had constructed for themselves over the previous year. She was in line ahead of me with a group of friends and, in one of those moments you wish weren't so memorable for being so rare, caught my eye and held it. Sparks passing in a glance like that can give a person an instantaneous overabundance of confidence. She had a stick of face paint prearranged in the shape of the Spanish flag, and I asked her to paint one on my face for the match.

We would continue to cross paths for the rest of the day. She even rushed over after a goal and gave me a peck on the cheek. I'm kicking myself as I write this because I was still deeply inhibited by a lifetime of conservative shame, not to mention the friends who were watching the match with me. How inhibited, you may be asking? WELL…

The Spanish win. We all make our way down to the waterfront where there's a fountain surrounded by a massive pool. The Swedish woman strips to her underwear, hands me her clothes, and prances back into the water with a look that still makes me dizzy seven years later.

And you know what I did? I HANDED HER CLOTHES TO HER FRIEND AND WENT HOME. Because that's what you do when you live on a vessel of judgment mischaracterized as "the Love Boat." I was too scared to jump in the water with her, especially in front of a bunch of other Mercy Shippers, and now you know the story of why I don't live in Stockholm today.

I need to go for a walk.

THE FREETOWN JITTERS

Our first screening day in Freetown was obviously traumatic. It's not how I suggest opening any new chapter in life, let alone in a new part of the world. I hardly left the ship for months afterward if I could help it. Any trip outside the port set my heart pounding. We had a second, much more successful screening day in a smaller, more controlled location, and I volunteered for overnight security. I also got picked by our off-ships security officer (one of those Special Forces guys I mentioned earlier) to act as our managing director's personal bodyguard. This resulted in no small amount of ribbing from my friends. Our MD wasn't thrilled by the idea either.

But we had ten months in Freetown, and over time my screeching anxieties faded into a dull hum. Recalling the events from that day would cause me to break out into a sweat for years to come, but I learned how to function in the city and came to really enjoy it. I even managed to publish my first finished novel. Writing on the ship was a challenge that developed an unlikely discipline: writing in any environment.

If you can imagine trying to write in a busy café where everyone feels perfectly comfortable sitting at your table and starting a conversation with you, or with whoever is nearby, regardless of how big your headphones and "leave me alone" death stare may be, you've got an inkling of the setting. Somehow, I managed to maintain some level of writing regularity.

White Shores, the first book in my *Vitalis Chronicles* fantasy trilogy, was released at an epic launch party on my birthday. The party itself was put on by a number of friends on the ship, organized by two in particular, Liz and Dulce, and remains one of the best memories in my publishing career to date. It was one of the things that made my time in Freetown truly special. My job, however, was the worst.

I didn't get hired on to make videos, as you might remember, and then once I got to the ship, I was approached about joining the team to make videos. But by that time, I'd seen the dysfunction of the communications department on full display and opted to stick with my job of running soundboards and keeping the ship's TV systems working. This wasn't necessarily a mistake; it was just an unfortunate choice out of two bad options.

I hated my job. Partially because it was inherently boring to me—just because you CAN set up a stage doesn't mean you're made to set up stages—and partially because it set me right in the middle of about a dozen crosshairs. Like a parabolic focal point of professional ire. I very quickly became the whipping boy for

a lot of the ships' leadership, who saw any technical error during one of their presentations as a personal affront. Never you mind the fact that we were working with a jumbled mess of equipment through which even Dr. Frankenstein would have hesitated to run electricity.

A big part of my job was organizing volunteers from the crew to run the soundboard and slides for the music's lyrics. That way, I wasn't pulling an extra ten hours of work a week going to rehearsals and every major meeting. A few poorly timed issues (half of which were user errors to begin with) suddenly landed me with the obligation to attend every major meeting. I basically lived in the International Lounge, the ship's version of an amphitheater, and I came to loathe it.

What made it harder was that I genuinely respected these people. In other circumstances, I knew I would have liked most of them (and most would go on to become great friends), but at the time, I couldn't stand it.

One of my favorites (who will remain nameless) would find me on any given weekend and follow me around screaming, occasionally to the point that he would begin weeping with rage, because I hadn't switched one of the ship's four TV channels over to golf. No exaggeration. We had a system for signing up to have the channels switched to whatever you preferred, and you were allowed a certain number of hours per week. This both seemed to be beneath the crew member in question, and also somehow less efficient than verbally abusing me on a regular basis.

It was probably a combination of circumstances, stress, and who knows what else. Because with rare exception, I came to really enjoy all of the people who terrorized me as the audiovisual technician (the screamer and I would become friends on a golf course in Togo—he gave me the best piece of golfing advice I have ever received). But this was then, and it was hell.

SERVER ROOMS ARE COLD

I started looking into returning to the English teaching program I had done in Nice. I wasn't thinking of leaving the ship, I was committed, but I also knew I'd be stupid not to prepare a potential exit. I signed up and put Paris at the top of my list.

We left Freetown at the end of our field service and docked in Tema, Ghana, for a short refit between field services. I found myself lashed to the ship because, despite having Accra and all sorts of interesting places to visit on our Christmas break, a shocking number of the crew just wanted to stay on board and watch football. And the satellite dish, standing on a rusted-out tripod on the dock, was in constant need of adjustment in order to keep it aligned and functioning. The self-adjusting onboard version was way out of our budget. Thankfully, manual calibrations are cheap (if wildly frustrating). My friends would go off to see a movie or explore Accra, and I would stand on the dock realigning a satellite dish I would one day relish throwing in a dumpster. When I finally broke down in the ship's server room, crying in a corner behind racks of technology that hated me, I made the move to transfer to the reception department and got the heck out of the IT office.

Reception was more social and, thanks to its role in emergency services, carried a more central sense of responsibility. I was put in a mild management role over the team and proceeded to enjoy Lomé markedly more than I had enjoyed Sierra Leone. This is where my best motorcycle stories all come from (but those are for another book).

Being in reception means being trapped behind a desk in the crossroads of the ship because you're the first responder in case of fire. If there are two of you, one can walk away. If you're on your own, you can leave only when someone trained on the

fire panel is available to relieve you. This makes for some pretty drab nights on night shift. It also means that you're susceptible to a little over-socialization. It's worse for women because who knows what random guy is going to lean against the counter and talk endlessly at you. In this guy's mind, you aren't trapped. You're totally interested.

On a ship that's 75% women, it can happen to men occasionally, too. Even me (just suspend your disbelief for a moment).

ATTEMPT NUMBER TWO: A WOMAN IN UNIFORM

I had some solid chemistry with a woman who was a fellow receptionist on the ship. Even if I was still out of my depth when it came to pulling proverbial triggers, we had a lot of fun together. When you work with an attractive person in close quarters, and you have great energy generating a lot of laughs, things have a tendency to heat up. It's basic thermodynamics.

Now, this isn't to say that workplace romances are a good idea—especially when you live in the same metal box and share a lot of the same friends and common spaces. But c'mon, how could things go wrong?

To be fair, I had been severely burned by the woman I dated in Togo (there are some great stories in there involving first kisses, one of the aforementioned motorcycle crashes, and getting robbed at borders—again, different book), so at the time, I was decidedly skittish when it came to getting close to anyone. I was exhausted, burned out, and still a bit heartbroken. But she pursued me a little, which was nice, even joining me for the occasional nap in my cabin. Snuggles only (kick kick kick).

Fast-forward to the Canary Islands and I decided that I should man up and ask her out on a proper date. We had all of

Gran Canaria to explore from the relative discomfort of dry dock and I wanted to share it with someone. So, we picked a night where neither of us were working and made plans to head out for dinner. Things even leveled up when the Spanish national director offered us a ride out of the port and to the boardwalk in his car. Anyone who has had the pleasure of walking a couple of miles through a port to get back to civilization will immediately recognize this as a win, date or no.

The director pulled up to the boardwalk and stopped the car. I hopped out and held the door for the lady in question. She promptly swung it shut behind her. He started to drive off. My right index finger attempted to go with him.

There are moments in life where you can feel panic try to inject itself into a situation. Realizing you didn't put enough postage on the envelope when you filed your taxes, waking up an hour late for your first day on your consulting job, or suddenly spotting a spider right as you turn off the lights all come to mind.

This wasn't nearly as traumatic as any number of other situations in which I'd found myself, but having my index finger slammed in the door of a now-moving vehicle was certainly reason enough for a little adrenaline hit. She, however, freaked out. I calmly asked the director to stop the car, which thankfully he did. I asked her to open the door, the handle of which I couldn't reach on my own. After wiping the blood away to check the circular hole that had been punched in my finger, I asked the director if he would be so kind as to take me to the nearest emergency room.

He dropped us off and asked if we'd be OK (no hablo español), to which I confidently responded yes because why not. She was kind enough to stick around for a while but got hungry, as people do. She left me sitting in the ER holding my bloody-but-hopefully-not-broken finger in a hospital where I didn't speak the language and had no indication that I'd ever get seen by a secretary,

let alone a medical professional. I can't blame her, I was hungry too, but I can say that this may have killed the vibe.

WHICH WAY IS OUT?

I'd worked in reception for something like six months at this point and was more than ready to get on to Paris. My application to teach English had snagged me a job at (well, very close to) my first preference of Paris. This was the same English teaching program I had entered in Nice, TAPIF, which at eleven hours per week is more a cultural exchange than a real job. But it was a visa that could get me back to France for a longer stint. At the same time, I had an offer from Mercy Ships' global office to work as a copywriter and editor—which meant I could continue working for Mercy Ships while taking a break from the ship itself.

This was the perfect combination for the moment.

My dad had a role in training new crew brought him to the ship regularly, which was a rare luxury. These visits were always a perk for two reasons. First, it was time I got to spend with my dad, plain and simple. And this trip coincided with the end of my time on the ship, so we were going to get to leave together. The second was who he was traveling *with*.

One of the most exciting gossip-churning events we enjoyed as long-term crew was getting to meet the new round of freshly trained long-term crew. Short-term crew are great, don't get me wrong, but they're gone in a flash. It's the long-termers who form the core of your friendships and, of course, offer the most romantic possibility.

One of our jobs in reception was processing new crew of all stripes, which meant we got the first look (which was usually unflattering, considering the state in which many of them arrived—especially if they'd just finished a few weeks upcountry

somewhere—my buddy Josh nearly died on his training field service and was covered in bites from some bug straight out of a horror flick). We took photos, printed badges, stored passports, and got them to sign their lives away before giving them a brief set of safety instructions and sending them off to eat shrink-wrapped leftovers in the dining hall. You know, glamor work.

Personally, and this will come as a total shock, I was over it.

My dad was going to show up, I'd get through processing his new group, and then we could hang out. We were going to rent motorcycles and head up to the volcano. We were going to go see dolphins. We had some seriously magical father-son stuff to get going before I hopped a flight to Mercy Ships' headquarters in Texas with him to get ready for Paris. I had a visa to claim and a new chapter to start.

And then she walked on board.

Attempt Number Three: Last Moment, First Sight

Now, I know what you're thinking (KEEP THAT DISBELIEF SUSPENDED) because she never believed this story either, but I very distinctly remember seeing her come on board and my shell cracked a little. I thought she was beautiful in a way that should be captured in marble.

And that was it. I closed the crack in my shell as best I could and ground my way through processing the group. We took their passports, gave them their safety speech, and sent them off to eat cold leftovers.

My dad and I rode motorcycles up to the top of the volcano. We saw dolphins. We had a magical time. Then we left the ship, I thought, never to return.

Chapter Four:
I Actually Got to Paris

EDITOR IN SHEESH

My parents lived in Texas at the time that I left the Canary Islands en route for Paris. They had moved there to work at Mercy Ships' HQ, as my mom's illness was progressive and excluded her from long-term field work. My dad and I missed our flight in Madrid, got into an extended fight with the travel agent he had to use for all of his groups, and eventually made it to east Texas in August of 2012. It was a whirlwind of seeing friends, ending with a solid road trip with my hetero-life-partner Jeff.

At this point, Jeff was the confirmed bachelor of our duo. He had a completely different take on women than I did and, like many of my French friends would soon be telling me, believed that more than anything I needed to chill out and just go with whatever moments came my way. We'll get into this in more detail later, but I grew up fairly religious, and the tenets of waiting until marriage had been drilled into me despite not being what I really wanted. I still held to them. He saw the conflict it caused within me.

As the one who wanted to get married one day, I maintained that there was definitely a need to keep the pressure on in the midst of navigating the modern romantic minefield. Even if I'd wandered a little closer to letting someone in, I wasn't ready to give up all of my defense mechanisms at once.

"You have to love yourself first" became his mantra.

"Yeah, but I can get loved too in the meantime." I'm not sure how he kept from ever slapping me.

We toured Texas breweries in Dallas and Austin and returned to east Texas just in time for my farewell BBQ. Just under a month after leaving the Canary Islands, I was in Paris.

Let's pause here to enjoy the moment. I was in Paris! To live! *happy sigh*

All right, that was refreshing, but moving on.

I had two jobs: teaching English for the French government, and writing/editing for Mercy Ships Global. Writing for Mercy Ships was great. The English teaching was painful.

Not only because of the hour-and-a-half commute one way (walk to metro to RER D to bus to another long walk), but because my boss got seriously ill right off the bat and left no one in charge of me. So, my schedule, while set in an hourly sense, was rarely filled with students in advance. As I walked up to the prison-turned-high school in Sarcelles, it was a coin toss as to whether I'd teach anyone or spend two hours sitting in an empty classroom before making the return journey home. I hated it.

It did, however, provide lots of time to write. I carried a Moleskine notebook with me every day, praying for an empty classroom. When that wish was granted, which was more often than it should have been but not nearly as often as I hoped, I pulled out my notebook and steadily filled a small book on the history of magic in my world from the perspective of an anthropologist writing from near the end of it all (not that he knew that). I hand-wrote the entries with flourished titles and sketched out the different symbols and iconography that came to mind as I created a history from nothing.

And then on the days where students did show up, I had to carry out the exact same lesson with every class over the course of two weeks so no one would miss out. Never mind how often entire swathes of potential students just never showed up to begin with.

As far as work went, editing for Mercy Ships Global was a lot more fun. Bryce, the director, is a squirrelly saint. He's one of those guys living his best life on an international stage, and it's hard not to be inspired when you're around him for long. His personal goal at the time, for example, was to convert a portion of an island in the Caribbean into a resort for burned-out humanitarian aid workers. He's a stud. I don't think that he's ever gotten the chance

to deal with me when I was in an emotionally healthy state, but somehow, he's always been patient, generous, and kind with me.

The gist of the job was taking existing articles written by staff on the ship and editing them down into smaller and smaller chunks for broad distribution and translation. It was a fun job and came with its own challenges that helped hone new skills. It also regularly got me out of Paris to the office in Switzerland, which is a win by any metric.

What it also did was require me to read all of the stories being produced on the ship. The majority of these were patient profiles, looking at where an individual patient had come from and how surgery had changed not only their health but their life moving back into their community. And who wrote the best stories being produced on the ship? Yep, the exact woman you're thinking of, and if you weren't, then you've missed the thread to this chapter. Let's call her Élodie from here on out because it's my second-favorite French name ever. Élodie was a fantastic writer and I found myself checking in regularly on her blog as well as the stories she wrote for the organization. This is where I slowly got undone.

There are lots of clichés about beauty because it's something we chase in every aspect of our lives. It's what we want in our homes, in our cities, and even the food we consume. Studies have shown what it seems like we must have always known, which is that we're very directly influenced by the beauty of our environments. While there are subjective takes on beauty, it exists objectively in our world (or we wouldn't all prefer to stare at Paris over Pittsburgh). That said, it also only gets you so far.

If you endure rude service in a restaurant, stumble through a fresh patch of urine on your way out the door, and then get mugged on the Métro, you might start to hate Paris regardless of how beautiful it is. The same holds true for men and women—

beauty is what may draw us in at first, but it can only hold us for so long.

Her beauty struck me. Her writing is what got me. We had brief email exchanges as I worked with her articles, and I steadily became proud of her work (which was weird for having only met long enough to take her passport). But her written words solidified a deeper crush than I could have anticipated.

I made a quick trip to visit the ship in Guinea, bringing with me a load of treats for all of my friends on the ship. This was by far the best trip I ever made to the ship, as I got to play Santa/counselor for a week and then bounce. I even brought some small souvenirs to make sure no one got left out. Secretly, I was hoping Élodie would be there. Unfortunately, she was traveling when I visited, so I left her a little Eiffel Tower keychain with a note and packed off back to Paris.

WOOD FLOORS

I've lived in Paris twice now, and I did it wrong both times. Thankfully (I guess?), I did it wrong in different ways each time. In the first instance, I moved with two jobs, one with Mercy Ships and one as an English assistant in a French high school. The English teaching gig was how I got my visa. I figured that since I had the employment situation locked down, I could find an apartment on the fly.

I. Was. Wrong.

For those of you who have never tried to find an apartment in Paris, especially on your own and with little working knowledge of how the system works, it is hell. Even a working knowledge of the system only moves you up a few levels in the Inferno. People

with serious cash on hand, or whose jobs do the heavy lifting for them, can enter into a state of Purgatory. No one save for families of former French nobility ever even dream of Paradise.

There are entire books written about this—it is real.

I did not read those books. I was delightfully if tragically naïve. When I got to Paris, I had a friend whose uncle was opening a restaurant and, hard up for cash, foolish enough to rent me space in what might have been a twenty-square-meter apartment (200 square feet). A tiny space which he also inhabited.

This was an apartment whose doors could never open completely without bumping into another structural element. It had a toilet, yes, but one I had to step over to enter the shower, and so close to the wall that I had to sit at an angle to use it. A kitchen with enough elbow room to shrug (without emotion), and the two main rooms large enough to unfold a single futon (if you keep your books flush with the shallow bookcase). In other words, a standard Parisian apartment.

The deal was that I could sleep on the floor in the "office" for 250 euros per month as long as I was actively looking for a place to live. This seemed reasonable. Of course, the aforementioned futon was in his room. All the "office" had on offer for furniture was a stool and plain desk in the corner. The silver lining was that this arrangement left plenty of space to sleep on the hardwood floor, and thus, being no stranger to crappy sleeping conditions, I was set.

I was in Paris!

Just the idea set me vibrating across the splintery wood floor. Between working on my own books, teaching English, and writing/editing for the Mercy Ships Global office, I had plenty to do when I wasn't bouncing around the city sightseeing. But as I started looking for an apartment with a futon all my own, I ran into a problem. The French government wasn't going to pay me until

after two months of work—which still seems questionable to me today but hey, who really needs money?

And it was no problem, I reasoned. It would certainly make getting an apartment more difficult, but at least Mercy Ships was continuing to pay me. Right?

Well, eventually. In transferring my account to the new office, someone forgot to cross a t or carry a y or maybe send the right breed of carrier pigeon. Whatever happened, I was not in the payroll system anymore.

"Ha. Haha. Ha ha ha." That's a direct quote from the moment I found out that no one was paying me while living in one of the most expensive cities in the world.

FROM LOW BOARD TO FREE BOARD

Things only got worse for the first two months I lived in Paris. Not only was I living with a grumpy stress ball of a roommate, but in order to live up to our agreement, I had to go see apartments with no way to actually rent one if I found one. This wasn't initially a concern, as I figured the competition would undercut my efforts at every turn. I knew the drill by now: assemble a dossier filled with every possible personal document any human might have even the most unreasonable desire to see, make a dozen copies, line up at 6 AM with forty other people to see one moldy rat-infested apartment, leave a copy of said dossier FILLED WITH VERY PERSONAL INFORMATION with total stranger, hear nothing back, repeat.

In the cruelest twist of irony to date, possibly in my entire life, I found PLENTY of apartments willing to take me on. And not drafty, ratty apartments either. One was freshly refurbished AND had a distant view of the Eiffel Tower AND the guy straight-up said he'd take me on immediately. "Why, thank you, sir, if only I had money." Smile and cowboy-stroll away.

My tactic quickly turned to not searching and lying to my host about it. As much as I enjoyed being the first potential renter in the history of Paris to do the rejecting, I couldn't handle the look on the poor proprietors' faces. Also, spending hours a day in this futile dance wasn't doing my sanity any favors. I needed money.

Things were getting really tight. What savings I had quickly dried up (pro tip: volunteers on hospital ships don't make much to begin with), and even my baguette-only diet was starting to pinch. My parents, while unable to offer much help, were able to float me fifty euros here and there to keep me from starving. My French bank account (the opening of which is also a nightmare worthy of its own chapter in another book) came with a hundred-euro credit, which I immediately used for my ninety-something-euro Navigo pass out to my school in distant Sarcelles.

Despite all of the pay-free work, I did receive my teacher's pass, an ID card which allowed me to enter all of the state-run monuments and museums in France *for free*. I eventually met a kind Italian who "loaned" me a sleeping mat to take the bite out of the wood floor (I say "loaned" because I was still using it up until about a year ago). So, there was plenty of silver lining to my cloud.

At least until my roommate kicked me out for the night so his girlfriend could come over. While totally understandable, there's nothing quite like receiving a text at 10 PM asking you not to come home. And it wouldn't be the last.

DESPERATE TIMES CALL FOR DESPERATE BLOG POSTS

I won't lie, my payroll/apartment situation stressed me out. I started feeling miserable in a way that you are not supposed to feel in Paris, goshdarnit. WHERE'S THE MAGIC.

But I came to realize that the magic was there whether or not I felt it. Yeah, I was shacking up in the apartment of the personification of anxiety, but I had a roof over my head I could afford. Sure, I wasn't getting paid, but at least I had a pass to enter any state-run museums and monuments I wanted for free. That was a perk I did not take for granted.

I held off blogging about the whole experience (back when I blogged with a *b*) because I wanted my next post to be "I'VE DONE IT! I slew the dragon that is Parisian apartment hunting and hung its head over my new mantle." But that post only seemed to be further and further from me the longer I waited to write it. The dragon wasn't winning because I couldn't defeat it—it was winning because my blacksmith was withholding my lances for another month.

To be perfectly honest, I was embarrassed. I'd chosen this adventure for myself, after all. I had lived in France before and knew the ropes, and still I was getting nowhere fast. To make matters worse, I had no money. This was nothing new, as I had never had money to begin with, but getting caught in the open like this made that latent shame flare to new life. I wasn't about to broadcast it to the world.

It was about this time I also found out just how expensive locksmiths in France are when I came home, turned the key, and the lock died of old age on the spot. It cost 250 euros just to pop said door open. My temporary landlord was not pleased.

While I didn't end up on the hook for the eventual 800-euro bill (not joking), it only served as another spike to my financial anxieties. The situation was untenable, as was my ongoing silence on the matter. I needed to let go of my shame and I knew it. That didn't make it easy, nor likely to happen quickly, but one morning I woke up and, as happens with sudden bursts of perspective, realized I was being a total putz. I had yet to starve. My situation

wasn't truly dire, even if it was stressful and embarrassing. I was alive and surviving in the city I loved!

Hadn't I just spent two years serving people who would have killed for an opportunity like this? I won't go so far as to say I had literal flashbacks of my time screening patients or observing surgery, but the weight of that contrast was there, real, and deeply sobering.

I got up, sat at my computer, and pounded out a post wherein I detailed just how hard things had truly been, how I was struggling, and how I knew I was going to be OK because you know what—it was out of my hands anyway, so why whine about it!

I slammed my laptop closed (gently) and marched out the door (more emphatically). I had my pass to the Métro and another to the city's finest cultural offerings. I was going to the Louvre because it was there and, though I couldn't afford to buy a real meal, I could damn well afford a trip to the world's most famous museum for the day. So, I went. I wandered along what would become a regular track through the Louvre whenever I felt like paying it a visit (because life's too short to not smell roses or take advantage of free passes to the Louvre). I wandered, checked in on a few of my favorite paintings, and sat down in the middle of the Denon wing to soak it all in. Because it was mine. It was my life and it was amazing, looming homelessness be damned.

And in that moment, I suddenly felt like I should leave. I didn't have cell service yet (BECAUSE I HAD NO MONEY), and I felt the urge to get home and check for messages. I figured I had all the time in the world to come back and visit the Louvre, so why not give in to the urge and bounce? I hopped on the Métro, crammed into Line 4, and haltingly slid back out at Marcadet-Poissonniers, just around the corner from my tiny patch of wood floor.

The warped stairs creaked under my ascent, the new lock in the door giving with a satisfying series of clacks, and I was in. I walked straight to the oversized laptop that had accompanied me through three West African countries and crossed the equator twice by sea, and cracked it back open. As if I had expected it to be there, a message was waiting for me on Facebook, and it would change my life.

THE FREELOADER'S BACK FOOT

What I found in that fateful Facebook message wound up being more than your average lifeline. It was from my friend, Anne, who I had met in Togo less than a year before. As I wandered the Louvre letting go of my fears, she was sitting on her bed in her mother-in-law's apartment in Paris, reading my blog post.

They were on their way to London for a wedding, she wrote, and only passing through, but if I had time, she would love to buy me dinner and introduce me to her mother-in-law who had offered up her maid's chamber if I needed a place to stay. Of course she didn't want to impose, she knew it was last-minute, but they would be back in a few weeks if I had time then.

I'm not sure whether the prospect a place to stay or the concept of a real meal excited me more in the moment. Of course I wanted to meet up! I nearly kicked the room's lonely stool through the window in my rush to get out.

Kiki, the woman I would come to lovingly refer to as my landlady (she prefers "Adopted Grandma"—we finally settled on "Grandlady") doesn't remember our dinner quite the way I do, but she's admitted it sounds like her. She was lovely, tiny, shrewd, and intimidating. This isn't merely subjective—she wields power with her presence and I personally think she relishes it. She spent that meal studiously side-eying me, and offered the maid's chamber

(chambre de bonne, in French) with the understanding that it was a temporary arrangement until I found a more suitable place to live. I wholeheartedly (and full-stomachly) accepted her offer, and she said that I could move in once the electricity had been updated.

What I didn't know at the time was that in the twenty-five years that she had owned the place, she had never once let anyone use the chambre de bonne. She barely let anyone stay in her own apartment without her present. To an outside observer who had known her for decades, like Anne, the offer to let me stay hit with the suddenness and shock of a tectonic shift. To me, it was nothing short of a miracle, and one that would only grow with time.

Chapter Five:
Unrequited <3

ISLE OF BEACHED DREAMS

WHY DO WE DO THIS?

CONGOLESE KICKERS

My first stint in Paris was difficult but a blast. I had struggled to find a place to live and gone months without a paycheck, but once I started getting paid and found myself in my chambre de bonne, things took a turn for the amazing. For the first time in my life, I had enough money coming in that I didn't really have to stress about anything day-to-day. It wasn't a lot, but if I wanted to buy a pizza, I could buy a pizza and not freak out over the double helping of guilt. I still had student loans and some pesky credit card debt lingering from my first foray into adulthood, but everything was essentially covered.

The room itself was a different take on a chambre de bonne as well. For the uninitiated, traditionally the chambre de bonne is attached to an apartment so the maid in question can drift in and out as necessary to work in the kitchen, clean, sing rock ballads, whatever it is maids do. They're tiny and often located on the very top floor of a building which—next time you're in Paris— is why there are often rows of small windows protruding from the roofline of the buildings in the city.

Mine was located in a separate dormitory-style building altogether, thirteen square meters with a shower, sink, and bidet that didn't squirt water. So, a glorified urinal (that I removed as quickly as possible). I threw my little mat down on the floor in the corner, set my laptop on the fifty-year-old sewing desk, and settled into a wonderful turn in Paris.

I made friends with a group of Niçois kids my age ([nee-swahs] = people from Nice), which was ironic because I'd barely met anyone from Nice while living there. I really started settling into this international version of myself that I had struggled to define for years. I also had tons of friends come visit on their way to or from the ship, and some of my early videos on Paris were

born from the necessity of organizing how I got them around town quickly on layovers.

I also released the third and final book in the *Vitalis Chronicles* trilogy to little success. Or *no success* would be a more accurate way of putting it. The second had been released while in Togo, and this third installment received more buzz and external hype than any of the others. And yet, it flopped outright. It served as a stinging reality check, one that would force me to face the question of why I wrote.

"Make the money; don't let the money make you. Change the game; don't let the game change you," Macklemore famously said. Well, he said it at least. His album *The Heist* and its title track were instrumental in identifying and leaning into my mentality in this period. I had always wanted to be independent, and I loved doing what I did regardless of whether or not it succeeded.

Was I hurt that sales were miserably low? Yes.

Was I going to quit doing what I loved if no one showed up to enjoy it with me? No.

It was one of the vital lessons from this stint in Paris. Unfortunately, however much I loved the city and however much I wanted to stay, it wasn't to last.

If you're an American who has ever tried to find a way to live in France, you'll be familiar with the challenges. For those of you who aren't: *c'est pas facile.*

Without European citizenship, visas are challenging and often come with set expiration dates. Mine lasted the length of the school year and then I had three months to get out. I could have enrolled in school, but I didn't have any money for tuition, let alone the plane tickets to return to the States for the visa.

I was also getting a little itchy. Living on the ship had led to almost daily adventures, a heightened existence that engaged me

on almost every level every day. Life in Paris was lovely, but it was comparably easy and isolated. It was also lonely, going from life in a metal box with 400 people on the same mission to living in a brick box by myself.

And while life in Paris was easy, the bureaucracy was the true challenge. Without any clear road forward, nor any idea how to get a job that would sponsor me to stay (I was woefully underqualified for any such job), I was coming to terms with the need to leave. But heading Stateside felt like an even worse option—especially if it meant returning to Spokane. No offense to Spokane, but the thought of giving in to the tug of that whirlpool generated the same feeling you get on the edge of a moral failure.

It would cost me every penny to fly back to the US, and then what would I do? The bills wouldn't stop coming just because I didn't have any income. It turns out that bills are pesky like that. Student loans don't go away, even if you volunteer for years on a hospital ship.

Thankfully, on that Santa-esque trip I made to the ship in Guinea, I met the communications manager and she saw some potential in me. She rang me up one day and asked if I would be interested in becoming the ship's media liaison.

The media liaison was responsible for all external media teams coming to the ship to film or photograph the organization working in the field. Scott Pelley had come with *60 Minutes* while we were in Togo, and it killed me to be unable to help them film. This job was right up my alley, the only one in the organization for which I had any remaining interest.

I was craving a return to ship life and some semblance of adventure. I told her I'd do it, so long as I was given space to recover and rest between media teams. I'd seen others do the job and I knew how heavily overworked they were and how badly

they burned out. The job had a reputation of its own. She seemed mildly affronted that I would assume this to still be the case, but promised we would work things out.

I twisted on it for a while, debating the pros and cons with my family when they came to visit. I had burned out pretty badly the last time I'd been on the ship, as well as having been generally burned along the way. But the job was attractive for its inherent challenges and my complementary strengths. I missed elements of ship life and the community. And I preferred how the Lebanese prepared their shawarmas in Western Africa to Europe, so the Congo had to have a decent one on offer too. I decided to take the job.

I quickly realized upon arriving in the Canaries that this would also put me into regular, direct contact with Élodie as well. This hadn't been a motivating factor in the decision, but it came as quite the exciting perk once I woke up.

Socializing, however, was barely given a footnote on my new work-life balance sheet.

My job looked a little like this: wake up at 6 AM, gather the media team in question at breakfast. Take them down to the dock to film patient intake or physical therapy or whatever was on the schedule for the day. Maybe eat lunch. Go to the OR for surgery and scrub half of the team in. Take the second half of the team to the engine room, or bridge, or patient ward—wherever they needed to film that day and keep them out of trouble. Maybe eat dinner. Gather surgery team who should have left already but couldn't bring themselves to stop filming, return to the dock to film patient discharge, dancing, physical therapy, whatever's unfolding outside. Spend the entire next day out at the dental clinic or an eye screening. Get little to no sleep. Sweet-talk your way past irritated crew members, government officials, or random bribe-seeking police. Repeat.

In fact, over the subsequent five months I would work twelve-to-fifteen-hour days, every day, with maybe one day off every two weeks.

This isn't hyperbole—we did the math when I finally took a month off for Christmas and went back to the States. Those thirty days of vacation didn't even make up for the weekends I had worked. Despite being frustrated, I'll be honest: I was kind of impressed with myself. Not sure anyone else was, but hey, someone had to be.

This didn't stop me from working myself up into my own ball of stress through my steadily growing crush on Élodie. I don't know if you've ever liked someone enough for your lungs to threaten to implode and take your heart with them, but I have to believe that it's the origins of the word *crush*.

We hit it off really well, right from the start. She was even more beautiful than I remembered. She was clever, intelligent, and well spoken. And our senses of humor overlapped brilliantly.

I. Couldn't. Get. Enough.

Now, in looking back, I recognize a few things much more clearly than I did at the time (those of you who watched my daily vlog know I got to Paris single, so there's no spoiler as to how this ended).

I used to be an unrepentant romantic—she wasn't the first debilitating crush of my life, although I can only think of two others. Being a romantic isn't a bad thing but, as with all things, is only good in moderation. This is why *Romeo and Juliet* is so horribly mischaracterized as romance. If everyone dies at the end of your love story, someone overstepped.

No one died in this love story, but I was too persistent. There's a myth that I used to believe that was pressed upon me from an early age which looked at women as the person in the equation who needed to be persuaded into the relationship (thanks,

Disney). The circles I grew up in believed in "pursuit," the idea that a guy had to overcome a woman's facade of disinterest and prove himself worthy. This is taking the chase (fun) and turning it into the hunt (baaaad). There's a whole book's worth of material we could get into about how harmful this can be, let alone how long it took me to deconstruct it for myself (still working on it), but let's just summarize it all by saying I hadn't quite figured this out yet.

And I can also be fair to myself by saying there was still room for confusion with Élodie. The upper decks of the ship are open to the outside world, where it's easy enough to sit in the humidity and watch the ships in port come and go. There isn't any real privacy, you're still sharing with a few hundred people and an entire biosphere's worth of moths and mosquitoes, but it is a welcome change of pace. It's also an industrial port setting, but you can pretend the lights on the cranes and masts are stars and, if you can ignore the wafts of exhaust, it can feel momentarily romantic.

Over the course of our first few months in the Congo, our conversations in her office or on deck moved slowly from friendship towards dating. More often, they were debates about whether or not we should, with her on team "we wouldn't work" and me on team "we totally would." In revisiting this, I realize how painfully exhausting this sounds. But the heart wants what it wants; it isn't the one that has to deal with the ulcers, after all. And if there was a center of gravity for me on the ship, it was her office.

I'm not sure I'll ever have an objective take on the progression we made from friends to more-than-friends, up to the point that she kissed me for the first time. There would have been plenty of mixed signals under normal circumstances, but we were living in circumstances that did more than enough to add to the confusion.

The Road to Brazzaville

So, you'll remember how I wound up working fifteen-hour days for five months straight. All this while on a floating hospital ship in a central African port, earning no money, and stressing out over a woman I thought I loved more than life itself? Yeah. It took its toll.

In looking back on this period, I often think that if I hadn't been head-over-heels for someone who wasn't *quite* as interested, I would have been just fine. Or if my boss had taken my request for time off seriously and fought for me to have a few days to rest here and there, maybe I wouldn't have snapped. Perhaps my brushes with burnout would have been limited to perpetual shift swings in reception, or adjusting the satellite dish one too many times on the dock. Maybe I would have gotten to the end of the service with some pep left in my step.

Unfortunately, I have a bit of an Icarus thing going on when it comes to burning.

And somehow, in the midst of all this, I drafted my first stand-alone novel, *Dark Horse*. Don't ask me how. I let Élodie read it and I even found her notes on it not that long ago—her kind commentary on my writing still made me smile.

We had some good times.

I, however, hit peak overwork when I had to pick up film crews from the airport *before* dropping the previous ones off for their departure. By the time my long-anticipated Christmas holiday came around, I was on the verge of a complete breakdown.

The last team to visit the ship before my sweet Christmas freedom was a Swedish TV crew, the most experienced professionals to visit the ship yet. They were jovial, smart, and genuinely wonderful people. I wanted to strangle them by the time I got them to their hotel.

I was beyond exhausted and yet unable to sleep. Part of the deal we had struck was that the film crews would no longer be permitted to stay on board, in an effort to buy me some space. Before this agreement, I was quite literally at their beck and call at all hours.

Living on a ship, with nowhere to hide and a pager on your hip, makes getting some quiet time by yourself nearly impossible when people *aren't* actively looking to crash it. As I had raised this concern from the beginning, my boss took the complaints that followed as if I were crying wolf. I would respond by highlighting that I hadn't had a break in a month, and she would point to the calendar and say, "Well, there are no teams coming during this window in two weeks. Just make it to there and I'll give you a few days."

Never mind how much it rankled to be told I might get "a few days" as if it were a concession after having no weekends for a month. Invariably, that open window would get filled with another media team of some sort, and the perpetual work cyclone would continue. You can imagine that my trust in her might have waned over time.

As things got more serious and I eventually found myself thinking murderous thoughts about happy-go-lucky Swedes, I put my foot down and demanded a serious look at the situation with my boss. And, because I didn't trust her to do anything to actually help me, my boss's boss (BB).

After I sent those horrifyingly happy Swedes packing for the night, BB joined us in our shared office, calendar in tow. We agreed that I would finish out with this last crew but that my boss would take my pager overnight so I could sleep until 7 AM. As far as compromises go, this sounds insane to me now, but it was better than nothing and I was dying. I went to bed relieved, genuinely excited for the prospect of just one full night of sleep and no pager to wreck it.

The next morning, at 6 AM, my phone started ringing. The film crew were waiting to come on board, I was told, and why wasn't I answering my pager? I politely hung up the phone, then leaned against the bulkhead and roared.

I got dressed in a fury, stumbled up to reception and over to security, where I signed in the friendliest group of Swedes I have ever wanted to slap. I walked them in for breakfast, grinding my teeth at their slovenly banter. Their hateful excitement for life. Their disgusting relish for the day's work ahead.

I was very, very mentally fucked up.

I immediately left them to their breakfast and sought my boss, who was nowhere to be found. I stumbled across BB in her office. I lost it. I broke down to the point that I physically struggled to stand back up.

Seeing as she genuinely cared that I not completely fall apart, BB asked me to go see the crew physician before taking the rest of the day off. A day. . .off, you say? What a novel idea. She would take care of the team until my boss could be found and put back in charge of them. Then we would figure out how to proceed.

I floated down to see the crew doc in a haze, and he pretty much immediately asked me to stop working and take a bunch of pills to sleep. I told him I'd manage, thanked him for the sleeping-pill offer, and went back to my cabin. I was tough. I could get through this.

I don't really remember what it was that broke my pride on this one, but I do remember sitting in midships during some community event that I wanted no part of. I sat as far back in the corner as I could, needing to be around people but not wanting to interact with any. My buddy Ruben came and sat with me. He just sat, which was perfect. The world beyond that was enveloped in fog.

I think it was about this time that I fully realized just how screwed up I was. Sitting a few tables away with his family, the crew physician gave me a look and I nodded back. He wrote a work release and handed it over. I took it, grateful, and turned to walk towards my office. I didn't have to go far, as my boss was walking up the hallway already. I just handed her the slip and walked down to my room, where I collapsed and slept for the next thirteen hours.

I would sleep just about as long every day for the following week, up until the time I left for Christmas. During this time, Élodie started visiting more regularly. If there was any upside to crashing into the sun, it was falling back to her. She would sneak down the hall and join me in my cabin for a few hours, we would snuggle, make out, and eventually she'd sneak away again, leaving me to my catatonic existence. Suddenly, the only downside to my situation was that we were going separate ways for Christmas.

I packed up and flew to the States, debating whether I would ever return. Things fell apart between Élodie and me again over distance. I stayed in Paris for a bit and reconnected with my friends. She went to Texas while I went to Washington. Things chilled.

Literally and figuratively; it's flipping freezing in eastern Washington in winter, and I'd been living near the equator! But it was during this return trip, on which I didn't even recuperate my lost weekends, when I decided it was time to leave. One of my crewmates had offered me a job working as a consultant on electronic medical records (EMR) back in the States. It meant good pay and constant travel—which sounded like just what I needed to transition back to life in America.

I couldn't be a volunteer forever. Especially not with an organization that not only made me pay room and board but was happy to take my health as well. I started watching Flash videos on the EMR in question and reading up on its documentation. I thought that this would be the way I could support my writing,

keep traveling, and maybe give things with Élodie a real chance in the real world. She wanted to move to New York—and New York could easily serve as my home base if I was traveling full-time.

Still, she wasn't a fan of the idea of me leaving the ship a few months early. I'm still not sure if she felt like I was abandoning her or just jumping the queue.

I got back to the ship first and it seemed like we might not even really get together. When she did arrive, we fell back into our routine of sitting on deck, watching the ships in port, and debating whether or not we would work as a couple. It got so confusing that at one point, the double-talk became double-actions.

We went to one of our secret watering holes outside the port, and I only had enough money for one big Turbo King (a local stout with a leaping lion on the label) and some fries. We spent half of the evening arguing about our future, her saying we couldn't date and me saying we could. We argued the entire walk home. We made out in the port by a giant pile of trash, as one does in a port. I remember gently turning her at one point so she wouldn't see a massive rat scurry over the pile, as a gentleman does in a port. And later, she would reveal to me that she considered that our first real date and had kept the bottle cap as a memento.

She spent the entirety of what she considered our first real date arguing with me that we couldn't date. I can't insert that gif of Ryan Reynolds slowly facepalming into the text here, but you can imagine it now.

We had a lot of these non-dates that involved long debates and making out in the back of taxis (never again by giant trash piles and their massive rats I never told her about). I was heading back to the States. I was going to make more money than I ever had, get things ready, and we could give it an honest shot. She didn't think we would work because we came from different worlds, but even then, we started talking about a future together.

Her family and their circles were very far removed from my own, but I didn't care. I thought she was stellar—I'd fit in one way or another. She even gave me a lesson in formal dining etiquette, in case you were still confused as to what kind of "different worlds" I'm alluding to here. And to be fair to her, the internal conflict was very real. Could she go for what she wanted at the risk of losing what she knew?

Even then, as we talked about what it would look like to get married (!!!), the arguments continued. They would do so all the way into our final weekend in Brazzaville together, during my goodbye-weekend trip with a bunch of our friends. We snuck off on our own and had both the best and most miserable time together. It's amazing how much pain you can withstand when there's just the smallest promise of a return on your heart's investment.

I remember finding a local street party and sitting down for a drink, listening to the band as a group of kids swarmed her to have their photo taken. I melted a little in that moment and many more between. My heart strained under the pressure as much if not more. We agreed to give it a shot. And then I left the Congo and started another new job in another strange place.

Sailing to a variety of countries with Mercy Ships and holding an equal variety of jobs had been like reaching a small archipelago on someone else's ship. Each island held different people and cultures, different possibilities for my future. A peek across the horizon. The one populated by French settlers seemed to suit me best, but their homeland and lifestyle lay on the far side of waters I had no way yet of traversing. I needed to resupply and find a new strategy.

The island held by some industrious Americans showed the most promise for just such a refitting. At least that was what they claimed.

SWEET CAROLINA

A matter of weeks later and I would find myself in Greenwood, South Carolina. Not where you saw this story jumping, was it? I certainly hadn't.

Did you know they have a Waffle House? I'd never seen a Waffle House in my life! Since we're way off topic for a moment, did you know that FEMA rates the severity of the situation on the ground after a major storm based on whether Waffle Houses in the region reduce their service? The worse the fallout on the ground, the more the menu shrinks and the slower they are to reopen (Waffle Houses have generators on site). If they close completely, you might be screwed. That's how hardcore Waffle House is.

I had taken a job as a consultant for a particular brand of EMR in the midst of the massive transition the medical community was being forced to undertake. This transition was a giant mess for a lot of reasons, but on my first day in Greenwood, the only mess bothering me was the one I had created for myself.

It was on the voyage to the Congo from the Canaries, shortly after my first stint in Paris, when I made friends with a woman who sold me on the idea of taking this consulting job when I was ready to finish with Mercy Ships. She had been consulting on EMR for a while. The job required copious amounts of travel and made good money. She painted a nice picture but I wasn't remotely interested at the time. We were at sea, there were dolphins playing with the bow of the ship, and I was heading to a new country with a new job (that I knew I would genuinely love this time). Not to mention there was a woman on board on whom I had the largest crush imaginable. Taking a job, any job, back in the United States at the time seemed absolutely absurd to me.

Standing in an urgent care unit in Greenwood, staring at the EMR on which I had been very lightly trained, was not a life

circumstance I had foreseen. How lightly trained, you might ask? This was the first time I had actually seen the software in person.

In the transition from Mercy Ships to this new job, I had to study the software via old-school Flash videos, pass the subsequent quizzes, and get an in-house certification with the consulting firm before they. . .bent the truth. . .to potential clients and said I was a "subject matter expert." The only subject on which I was an expert was the length of time I had before the Starbucks Wi-Fi kicked me off.

Since the Flash videos were produced with ancient Mayan technology, there was no way to rewind them without entirely restarting. They lasted fifty minutes on average. Starbucks Wi-Fi lasted just under an hour per session. I wound up getting very close to the end of a lot of videos, but not quite finishing them, before the Wi-Fi reset and I found myself getting to start all over. While painful in the moment, it probably helped me learn the software better than I otherwise would have. That didn't reduce the pain of sitting in a Starbucks in Paris for a week instead of enjoying the city. The software itself was easy enough to learn.

It turns out that standing in urgent care, surrounded by suspicious doctors and nurses who had all actually used this software before, and supporting them in the midst of a live update is somewhat different to watching videos of someone else using the software.

Here are some tricks to consulting for the consultant who has no right to be consulting:

Rule Number One: Be liked. 80% of the job is getting people to like you. If they like you, they'll trust you, and even if they figure out how big the holes in your knowledge are, they'll be more likely to overlook them because they want to keep you around.

Rule Number Two: Try really hard to get the right answer without letting on that you don't have a clue. The best tactic

for this is saying "That's a great question! I haven't heard that one before; let me check real quick and I'll get back to you." While not ideal in emergent situations, this is a lifesaver. It shows initiative (at least, that's what you hope it shows). Call someone who knows better than you ASAP and then stroll back in with "Ah, yeah, duh. I figured it out. Here, let me show you real quick."

Rule Number Three: Always leave yourself outs. Never get visibly overconfident in what you're doing—first, ask them to tell you what they think should work and explain what they've already done (especially if their initial question sounded like gibberish). This prevents you from wandering straight into the same dead end in front of them.

If you see a fix, fix it. If not, commiserate over the state of things—you too are frustrated with this nonsensical change. It's not their fault they're confused; the software is what's ridiculous. This buys you some space to figure it out on the fly (especially if they like you!) and then, if you can't figure it out right away, get back to Rule Number Two by saying "I don't want to hold you up on this, I know you're busy, I'll go figure it out and be right back." Then sprint for the bathroom and make that phone call again.

I made a lot of bathroom phone calls. Thankfully, nobody died.

This was my first consulting gig and it lasted two weeks. Two weeks of being very much in over my head, but two weeks that established me in a job that would last for two years.

At least I didn't sink.

When I decided to take the job and make the early transition out of Mercy Ships, I had done so with three driving motivations in mind, three things I wanted more than anything: to travel, to write, and to be with a woman I had fallen for upon seeing her enter the ship in the Canary Islands.

Up in the Air

I soon wound up in Louisville, Kentucky, where I would be based for most of the next eight months. That's not to say I worked in Louisville the entire time, though I would do so frequently. An inordinate amount of time was spent traveling out to smaller towns in the region. Our employers were buying a lot of small clinics spread all over the region, which meant we would be supporting them during transitions from older software or straight from paper.

I learned a lot, like how to differentiate between a doctor who hated the new system because it was genuinely terrible and one who knew their long-term game of fraud was up. Having lived on board a hospital ship with surgeons for the better part of three years helped immensely when it came to not letting doctors intimidate me. Where my abilities had grown in interpersonal relationships in high-stress environments on Mercy Ships, this was different, as there was little to no real common ground between parties.

Our employers wanted to get them sufficiently trained and running on the software as quickly as possible. In turn, the clinical staff wanted nothing to do with the software or, by extension, us. To make matters worse, even among our own team of consultants, there was a lot of distrust and unhealthy competition. This was driven largely by the widespread abuse of funds one might expect when giant checks are being written to recruiters and overpriced consultants like myself.

Unfortunately, my brief career started after the golden era of massive per diems and minimum oversight. But I still got to hear the stories.

It was into this stress cluster of a situation that I found myself faking my way through my daily existence. We would fly in

on Sunday night, work in a random clinic for four ten-hour shifts, and then fly home on Thursday afternoon. All of the airfare, hotel, food, and rental car were paid for by the client. The expenses often matched our salaries, especially since we never bought airfare more than a few weeks in advance.

As I didn't have a home of which to speak during this era, I used this weekly airfare to visit friends all over the country. This was a perk for a number of reasons, not least of which was getting to see more of the country than I ever had the chance while growing up.

But even better was being treated like a guest of honor every weekend. If people don't see you for months at a time, they'll go out of their way to make time on the one weekend they get. I bounced between cities, crashing on couches and in guest rooms across the country. Family in the Northwest, friends in Boston and Chicago, and my buddy Jeff's family in LA—which was weird because he, the confirmed bachelor, had started dating someone and it was looking serious. But hey, I was living quite the life, wasn't I? If attention and quality time are what you're after, it definitely beats living anywhere permanently. Over time, one might realize that it's still nothing compared to consistent community.

I had two years to figure this out. In the meantime, I would frequently be asked if I'd ever seen *Up in the Air* with George Clooney. I would respond that I didn't know George Clooney. *Starring* George Clooney, they would clarify. Oh, I would say, no, I hadn't. I would then be warned not to watch it until I quit my job. This wasn't unwise advice, as I recently watched the film for the first time and thought, "Wow, I'm glad I'm not that guy anymore."

But before I would fall too deeply into the hole that was accruing points for airline status and forgetting what city I was in every time I woke up, I had Kentucky to conquer. What was most exciting about Kentucky was the anticipation of exploring it with

Élodie once she got off the ship and returned to the States. Our last few weeks together had taken a sharp turn for the better, and it seemed for a while that it would maintain that trajectory over distance.

KENTUCKY LIVING

Louisville isn't limited to fancy hats and baseball bats. There are some really great places to hang out, like this restaurant that makes eggs Benedict on corn bread with queso-instead-of-hollandaise that I still dream of. If I had been there doing something I cared about with people who weren't actively trying to get me fired, I think I would have enjoyed myself.

Life on the road is lonely. When I got into the EMR job, I really wanted to keep traveling. This was partially because I had learned so much from seeing the world and I didn't want that experience to stop. It was also partially because I was on the run.

If you followed my vlog for any length of time, you might have heard me talk a little bit about my time back in my home state, Washington. Breaking the gravity well around where I grew up in Pullman was really challenging.

When I set out for film school, I had my sights set on USC in Los Angeles but wound up at Eastern Washington University when the realities of cost settled in ($40,000 per year versus $5000 per year at that time). When you're headed to college with no help from anyone, bigger numbers get scarier quicker.

I had fun at Eastern but I wasn't challenged. Not personally, and certainly not educationally. I struggled in high school to keep up a 3.6 GPA but slept through my first 4.0 at Eastern.

What I came to realize while stewing in this pool of my own mediocrity was that not only was I not progressing towards

the movies I wanted to make one day, I wasn't really doing much to prove I was capable of it.

OK, rewind. In reality, I wasn't aware of this yet; I just thought it was unfair that so few people saw the same potential in me that I saw in me. I would come to realize *later* that I simply hadn't been giving them much to look at. This is a sense of entitlement that would get bashed violently out of me in the midst of the recession a few years later (but you know all about that).

Even then, I didn't feel like I really belonged. I wanted to get to France, speak new languages, and tell stories for a living. The battle I had yet to truly face was with my pride. The reality was that I was also surrounded by a lot of people who didn't understand my dreams and, rather than encourage me to figure it out, did what they could to re-form them into something they could understand, or dismiss them altogether.

This was what Spokane came to mean to me. Doubly so after living in Nice for a year and returning. People who were supposed to be my mentors actively cut me down when I tried to relate my experiences. I was told more than once that my aims in life were too high, that "not everyone is called to sexy places like Paris." I should be happy where I was. I should get a job I hated, save up for a retirement I'd probably die before seeing, and do so while hitched to some woman I never liked popping out kids I never wanted.

Now, I felt like I'd been fortunate to show at least a little bit of what I was capable of. After spending three years living in multiple countries, working alongside Lords of Parliament and meeting TV personalities, ambassadors, and presidents, I felt like there were people who had seen me operate at the top of my game. People I respected who respected me in turn.

Going back to Spokane would feel like admitting defeat.

To be fair to the people back in Spokane, it was more an issue of perspective. But at the time, I wasn't strong enough to take the misunderstandings or passive rejections.

So, I took the only sensible out when I needed to bail on Mercy Ships and hopped a plane. And then another plane. And then so many more planes that in 2015, I flew 116,000 miles. Domestic.

I was on an airplane every three days, multiple as I had to get to some pretty remote places (ever been to Baudette, MN?). I did not want to go back to Spokane. Ever.

But I did visit, as my sister was still there at the time. Eventually, my parents would leave Texas and move there as well, reducing my time spent in Dallas–Fort Worth's airport and restoring more power to the gravity well. There were and are some great people in Spokane; don't get me wrong. One of my favorite pizzas in the world was created there. But spending extended periods of time there, back when I was still raw from previous escape attempts, steadily crushed me.

So, I hopped plane after plane after plane. I earned the highest status American Airlines had to offer, racked up the hotel points, and on and on it went as my soul eroded under a different kind of pressure.

It would get much worse over time, but when I arrived in Louisville, I had only just gotten my first taste.

Most of the team I worked on had been doing the EMR game for a long time and, while sometimes neurotic, were out to protect the whole team. Of course, I got paired up with the one person who seemed ready to throw anyone under a bus at the first scent of trouble. We strolled into new clinics every week and, as I walked on eggshells with my coworker, would proceed to dance on the eggshells of a new office with its own politics and, often, loathing for what we represented. All of this with our hiring

manager breathing fire down our necks from the get-go (pretty sure he had an Accuse! button between Reply and BCC).

At the very beginning, I was proud to be figuring out this entire new world and earning more money than I ever had, because I was doing it with someone else in mind. There was a good chance Élodie would move to New York when she got back, and with this job, it would be easy to stay with her on the weekends and pay my way towards a new start. I could start putting down some roots, get centered, and maybe recover from two of the most outrageous periods of my life.

LONDON BUT NOT ENGLAND

I make a lot of recommendations. It's part of my job now. Starting a new high-stress job straight out of burnout isn't one of them.

Unfortunately, many of us don't really have an option, considering that money doesn't grow on any of the trees we have yet to come across (unless you're holding out on me). I certainly didn't have another option. What kept me going was the excitement of it all.

I had a job that paid for airfare and hotels, rental cars and meals. I had to wear a suit, which was simultaneously cool and obnoxious (my first few suits were terrible). And I got to share the whole experience with this beautiful woman on a ship in Africa, all with the expectation that she'd join me soon after. Our relationship even seemed to improve significantly during this initial phase. We argued a lot less, made plans for her return, and at one point, her dad even wanted to fly up to meet me (!!!x10 + terror emoji). She nixed that one.

I got my first gig almost immediately, relieving the stress of uncertainty while adding the stress of "Holy crap, I've gotta

go pretend I actually know what I'm doing for money now."
Greenwood came and went with its stress and awkward moments.
I got my second gig quickly as well, another relief as I prepared
to fly to Louisville. It was in the middle of the Kentucky Derby,
an event with which I was woefully unfamiliar—if you are too, it
happens to be quite popular. The only flight left was a $2,092 first
class round-trip fare. It was a ticket from Tyler, Texas to Louisville,
Kentucky, a distance of about 770 miles, and was the most I have
ever spent on a ticket to anywhere ever.

Welcome to the insanity of my new life.

I didn't know what you were even supposed to do in first
class. Could I ask for more snacks? Would there be champagne?
I figured it was best to keep my mouth shut and do whatever the
other passengers were doing for fear of being discovered and
shoved into the fuselage. Élodie had flown first class, so I asked
her questions about it instead. She asked if I'd go to the Derby—I
wasn't sure I'd be allowed on the grounds.

Kentucky was stressful for the reasons we've already
discussed. I was still green and faking my way through every aspect
of the job while the people who hired me were actively trying to
sniff out any consultants they could get rid of. I had a teammate
who seemed more than willing to help them. I wrecked a rental
truck early on and wiped out my savings (why is this a theme in
this book?) because it was one of the few vehicles not covered by
my insurance, a hard and fast lesson in reading the fine print on the
insurance offered by your credit card. And through it all, I could
feel my relationship with Élodie slipping.

Who knows how much distance played into this, or the
oncoming reality of her return to the States, or perhaps I was a
total ass on the phone (I can think of a couple qualifying moments
as I write this). Do we ever really know why these things burn and

fade the way they do? If our own hearts are mysteries, then the hearts of others must be absolute enigmas.

There was nothing I could do to stoke that flame again, try as I might. We danced around it for weeks. I got sent to random, remote clinics in rural Kentucky. She started to talk about how she wasn't sure she'd come visit me right away when she got back. I stood in the window of my high-rise hotel, staring out over a darkening Louisville, and felt like I had set myself adrift on a doomed voyage.

It wasn't a shock. At least, not in the sense that shocks are surprising. It started out slow and subtle, but she had frozen me out before. I saw the signs.

I got sent out to London, Kentucky, which is located in one of the prettier parts of the state. It's hilly there, with rocky outcroppings covered in thick trees. It reminded me of home, if Washington had humidity and horses with pedigrees.

We were set to work between there and Corbin, the town where Colonel Sanders started selling his famous fried chicken by the side of the road. They were smaller towns. The hotel we wound up in was three stories tall and consisted of one wing, a lobby in the middle, and a swimming pool you could smell through multiple closed doors. In other words, a simple box.

I took a room on the top floor. There were plenty of country roads to run, and my Fitbit was hungry for those 10,000 steps. If I did, it would reward me with a happy set of lights and vibrations like tiny digital fireworks on my wrist. I tried to get my angst out that way—at least my Fitbit could find fulfillment.

I got out of the clinic one day and left in the midst of a pounding rain. The air was oversaturated, sticking as I got in my rental car and sloshed away. I got back to my hotel, flopped onto the bed, and called Élodie six time zones ahead. It was a familiar

conversation, rooted in our former will-we-or-won't-we-work? But now, rather than straight-up saying it was over, she was waffling on coming to visit me.

She forced my hand. I told her that if she didn't come to Louisville as promised, we might as well be over. She said she wasn't going to come to Louisville. I said *All right, then,* she said something as flat, and I hung up the phone.

I lay there staring at the ceiling for a while, listening to the rain as it pattered angrily at the window. I don't know how long I searched the ceiling, but eventually I got anxious, itchy, craving a run but not wanting to set foot in the storm. I got up and walked out into the hallway, the door clicking behind me with a soft thud. The stairwell was a couple of doors to my right. I turned left and walked to the end of the hall, then down the opposite set of stairs. I walked back along the length of the hotel, passing the vending machines, ice maker, and empty swimming pool before walking back up to the third floor to complete the loop. I did this again, head hung low, watching my feet. And again. And again.

I kept walking through that hotel, making slow laps until my Fitbit vibrated its callous song and dance. I returned to my room, threw myself on the bed, and went to sleep.

CHAPTER SIX:
CONSULTING TO ITN

WORK TO LIVE OR WORK TO WORK?

I may have been steadily sliding into what would be the darkest period of my life, but I didn't do so without my usual sense of optimism for a future that, apparently, only I could see. There were three legs to the table of life I was hoping to build: storytelling, travel, and doing both with someone I loved. I was as far from the third as possible, but the other two were off on roaring adventures of their own.

Travel was so deeply ingrained in my lifestyle that I flew more regularly than most airline pilots. You've hit a new level of tolerance for the weird when you don't think twice about everyone working on any given plane knowing your name. When a flight attendant snaps at you in frustration before looking at the manifest and returns with five bottles of whiskey, a wink, and a smile, things aren't normal. Still, writing is what took the most interesting turn at this point.

While working for Mercy Ships, I self-published the *Vitalis Chronicles*, a fantasy trilogy, and drafted a fourth book, *Dark Horse*, before carting myself back to America. Throughout all of this, sales and exposure steadily declined with the release of each book. The golden era of self-publishing on Kindle had passed, at least in an algorithmic sense, and I couldn't reach readers on my own. I needed to do something to grow my own audience to support my addiction for my stories. But what?

Even if you're unfamiliar with audience building and retention, you're probably aware that it's not easy. If you think it looks easy, give it a shot. Either way, you might be surprised to learn how much more difficult it is to build one purely around your writing. This is largely because writing isn't easy to share.

Blogging of any kind takes time. The rule of thumb that I think still holds true is that you need to commit to creating regular

content for a minimum of a year. You also want to stick to your original strategy for the first six months before you think about making big changes. That time is necessary to see if it's working or not, largely because it takes a while for anyone to find you, and even more to decide they'll stick around for the long haul. The two main ways anyone might discover you are through search or recommendation. Months are required, at a minimum, for those things to start happening reliably.

The major difference between fiction and nonfiction in this arena is that fiction isn't broadly searchable, and it's even less broadly shareable. These struggles plague even the news: most people only read the headline, and few will click through to read the article itself. If you find a funny cat gif, you can send that to your friends or retweet it and everyone will enjoy it in the time it takes to watch. If you read a short story and send that to your friends, they'll thank you for the homework.

Reading, as compared to music or photos or videos, comes with a very high barrier to entry. In order to know if I like a song, I only need to listen to the first few bars to tell if I'm interested. I'll know if I want to watch a video on YouTube within seconds. Pass me a novel and it could be thirty minutes before I figure out who the protagonist is, and I have to do all the heavy lifting of imagining what she looks like.

This isn't to sell books short. I love books. I write books (hello!). Books simply don't go viral like other mediums without significant groundwork and lots of hype. And if I was ever going to make movies out of the stories I was writing, I would need a big audience and some money to boot.

I was trying to figure out how I could write something that would both build an audience over time and have elements within it that could be shared. I needed serial content but with viral components. I thought about sharing worldbuilding ephemera

that I had written over the years, but that seemed too rife with potential spoilers and unfinished details. I considered sharing the parables and myths I was working on from within my world, the brief histories and back stories behind the magic and the people wielding it. But that was way too niche. I mean, parables? This was the kind of stuff people might be into *after* they were invested in the world. It wasn't a way to *get* them invested.

I stewed on this for years. I wrote all kinds of things that never went anywhere. Then I stewed some more.

During my last few days in the Congo, we met up with some guys we knew who had their own shipping company that specialized in getting beer from the port in Pointe-Noire all the way upcountry to Brazzaville. This sounds simple enough until you realize that there was hardly a road between the two when they got started. Their stories were amazing if not a little harrowing, involving government corruption, dragging trucks from overnight swamps, and surviving literal gun-toting bandits. They were never a disappointment. One of them pointed me towards a book called *Blood River,* which chronicled a journalist's attempt to recreate Stanley's discovery of the Congo River in the modern-day Democratic Republic of Congo (DRC). The history, he said, combined with the contrast of pre-colonial Congo to today's DRC was staggering. I had only seen Kinshasa, the capital of the DRC, from across the river in Brazzaville. I was intrigued.

I picked the book up Stateside, started reading on my parents' couch in Texas, and put the book down before finishing the introduction. This was it. This was the story I wanted to tell that could be serialized and shareable. Not a masochistic journalist out to risk his life along the Congo River for the thrill of it. But the journal of a man exiled into the world's most hostile jungle, in search of someone he hated, and with no real hope of surviving. Someone fallen from the pinnacle of society, who needed to face

his own pride and self-righteousness in the outrageously lethal jungles of the Nanten. It could have illustrations and be released one entry per day, in real time. I nearly vibrated off the couch and onto the floor.

Rather than explode, I immediately got in touch with Nimit Malavia, the artist who had done the cover for my third book, and pitched him the idea. I'd always wanted to do something bigger with him, but I'd never had the right idea nor the money to fund it. Now I had a job and an idea. Now was my chance.

ON THE ROAD AGAIN

Sometimes, I wonder how many people in the world live the way I did during this period of my life. Not necessarily on the road, but locked in repetitive isolation. Get up, go to work. Don't really do much work because your job is a joke. Go home alone. Exercise or eat or watch TV before sleep. Repeat.

How many people around the world are on autopilot? Showing up because they have to. Going home to no one in particular or no one at all. Wishing they could change it but feeling powerless to do so.

The job I had in Louisville sent me all over the Midwest to clinics in places I would have otherwise never visited. I worked in the cornfields of Iowa and on the Canadian border with Minnesota. From North Dakotan oil fields to towns that, honestly, could have been in Kentucky or Indiana for how many times we crossed the river to get to them. I bounced around endlessly, from hotel to airport and airplane to rental car. I supported medical staff that didn't really need me, ate bland meals at empty diners that didn't really see me, and always wound up in boxy rooms through which I was merely passing. The weekends I spent in Chicago or Boston or LA were regular touchpoints with people who loved me, but I

was always back on a plane before I had a chance to leave a wrinkle on a pillowcase.

On the outside, I think I loved it. It made me feel somehow important to get flown all over the place, to have my meals paid for and free car rentals accruing in the background. On the inside, I was trapped, and I didn't know how to reverse course.

The benefit to being on the road is that you can stay a step ahead of the self you want to leave behind, at least for a while. New faces every week means the same standard questions. You impress people enough that they give you a good report, you dodge any meaningful conversations, and you turn in your rental car before it feels like it belongs to you. The downside to all this is that when that self you're fleeing inevitably catches up, and it will, you're likely to be alone in the middle of nowhere. This is not where you want any chase to end.

The middle of nowhere for me was Springfield, Illinois.

HARDER NOT SMARTER

We dove into *Into the Nanten* with relish. I wanted it to be a writing experiment as much as anything, to give the audience a chance to interact with it and possibly influence the narrative as it unfolded. I still had to get plenty written in advance; otherwise, Nimit would never have had time to make the art. Things tended to cut a little close as it was.

The goal was to publish every day, with an average of three illustrations per week. Playing with the timing of the posts was one of the best parts, posting them at night or in the morning to correspond with the time they were written in the jungle. If the characters were in trouble, running for their lives or hiding underground, there would be no post that day. Tension would build until finally, a new post: "I can't believe what just happened

and neither will anyone reading this." The idea gave me tingles.

This, I thought, was going to put me on the map. Somewhere. Someone had to notice. I kept two months ahead with my writing, hoping Nimit could keep at least a month ahead with the illustrations and provide us with some buffer. It was a lovely dream.

One of the defining features of the experience became stressing over whether the art would be finished in time. Aside from that it was a great experience. Nimit is wildly talented, as is instantly evident to anyone browsing his portfolio. Entrusting him to bring the world to life through the vignettes of journal entries was satisfying in its own right. The weekly art dump in my Dropbox generated a weekly squeal-fest. At the time, it was one of the few parts of my life I enjoyed.

We started gaining readers. They trickled in and I thought to myself, *Just keep this up. All you need is to get discovered by the right person.* I figured meeting potential readers face-to-face could give me a boost. Thanks to my practically unlimited weekend-travel-package, I started booking myself into sci-fi and fantasy conventions wherever I could. This started, ironically, in Spokane, where one of the biggest SF/F conventions was to be held that year: Worldcon. Or as you might have called it as wildfire smoke descended over the city: ApocalyptaCon.

As I wasn't about to be invited to speak or sit on a panel anytime soon, I entered with a two-pronged approach: I volunteered to help with setup and, just in case I made no friends that way, I bought my way in. The only way this was possible at my level (and budget) was by hanging art in the convention's gallery and taking a table in the Artists' Alley. I made a full presentation of a booth, printed a large-scale map of the Nanten on canvas, brought art in various formats to share and sell, and printed and hung large format pieces in the gallery. I even framed a massive version of the

cover of *Dark Horse* in a big, black, rustic old frame that looked fit for an abandoned castle. I was ready.

It was a lot of work. Volunteering before the convention opened was made possible by taking a little time off. Staying with my parents for free didn't hurt either.

My experience throughout life has been that if you're generous, you're more likely to make friends. Give without expectation and hopefully someone out there will spot you doing so and declare you their buddy (because who *doesn't* want givers for friends?). Unfortunately, in this instance, my theory failed. I didn't make any friends through volunteering to build displays and drive organizers around on errands—which seems really counterintuitive to me, but they weren't particularly interested in socializing.

At the same time, especially after living on the ship for a few years, I get it. They put on dozens of these conventions together all over the country, and as when entering any group of long-term volunteers, I'd have to pay my dues. Like *come back four more times and we'll talk* dues. While it was a swing and a miss on that front, it was still satisfying to stretch my old volunteering muscles a bit. We filled the massive concrete space with art, a bar, costume-repair stations, and more wizards' hats than you can shake a wand at.

And once the convention started in earnest, the sociability rating shifted dramatically. My booth, and the Reddit Fantasy community in particular, very quickly provided new friend opportunities. The Reddit moderators on site were kind and very generous in their own right, treating me to an opportunity to run an Ask Me Anything during the convention and introducing me to all kinds of people along the way.

I met my buddy Mike for the first time by their recommendation, and he too led me around, making introductions and inviting me into dinners and drinks I felt unqualified to attend. And then Auntie's Books, an independent bookstore that carried

my books for a time, made the crazy gesture of inviting me to the Hugo Awards Losers' Party.

Now, at first glance, an invitation to a losers' party doesn't sound particularly generous, but I should explain that, to my understanding, the Hugo Losers' Party is *the* party to attend after the Hugos (arguably the Oscars of sci-fi/fantasy). This is because the winners' party is a very small and exclusive event. 80% of the people nominated for an award wind up at another location for their own equally exclusive party, along with their agents, publishers, and friends.

This means that the party is loaded with interesting people and, eventually, the winners always join in after they've had their moment apart. This year's party was hosted by Auntie's Bookstore, the only non-pizza-related retailer in Spokane I'll unflinchingly promote. It was amazing. George RR Martin even rubbed his belly on me (which, unfortunately, resulted in no notable uptick in my fortunes).

I left that party on a cloud. I knew I wasn't one of them in the sense that I hadn't yet earned my place, but I had seen a glimpse of what could be my future. I just had to figure out *how*.

NOT THE ONE FROM THE SIMPSONS

Springfield, Illinois is famous for being Abraham Lincoln's hometown. That's about it. It's certainly a decent claim to fame; you'll stumble across any number of Abe impersonators wandering the streets, complete with all the height and gravity of the man himself. But aside from the Presidential Library, there isn't a whole lot to see or do. Impersonators included (they tend to focus on the dignity of the man and forget the humility, in my experience, which is such a weird sentence to write out, but there it is).

I wound up very, very bored in Springfield, working

what would be my last EMR contract. It was a contract that was supposed to last a few months but continued getting extended until we were there for nearly a year. There were three different health care organizations joining in on the project, which meant three times the potential for conflict and delay.

They really should have let us go until they were ready to launch. We were expensive and unnecessary. They didn't let us go, however, because they were worried we would get picked up by another client in the interim, thereby leaving them high and dry from a staffing perspective. What they didn't realize was that work was drying up everywhere and we would have just wound up unemployed.

We let them believe we were in high demand.

There's nothing that demoralizes quite like having a job you hate where you aren't even doing the thing you were hired to do, which you hate, but you're still under threat of getting fired for not doing anything, which, you guessed it, isn't great. It sucks the life out of you pretty quickly. Throw in a couple of coworkers who turn that anxiety into busywork, and you've got yourself some good old-fashioned forty-proof misery.

Thankfully, there were a couple of coworkers who were content to make themselves more obvious targets for being fired through various means. This meant I was able to sit squarely in the middle, not really doing anything but not standing out for it, either. This is not how I normally try to live my life, but for once, it seemed the most prudent course.

And it wasn't that I wasn't doing *anything*; I just wasn't really doing anything I had been hired to do. I was flying in every week and then sent to a windowless box to stare at my computer and wait for my lunch break. There was occasional work, but I didn't offer to make myself unnecessarily busy beyond that, because none of the work generated in these moments went anywhere. Busywork

for busywork's sake is worse than being left to your own devices.

What I spent my time and energy on, sitting in that windowless box with my laptop and a bunch of other equally underutilized consultants, was *Into the Nanten*. I was on the verge of completing my first season and I wanted there to be a second. What better way to get people energized and fund the project than a Kickstarter campaign? Running a proper campaign takes months of preparation and an ungodly amount of work (let's be honest: we took some shortcuts on the one that brought you this book). Thankfully, I was getting paid to sit around and do nothing all day, so I had my chance to do due diligence.

It was a little tense at times because, ever the honest soul, I didn't hide what I was doing and our supervisor made the occasional quip. But she didn't really mind because what else was I going to do?

I made it clear I was available and ready to roll. Would she rather I stand in the corner trying to breathe quietly and avoid attracting an overabundance of dust? She read my fourth book, *Dark Horse*, at some point and enjoyed it enough to intrigue her (Rule Number One of consulting works in more ways than you might think). We settled into a decent equilibrium.

I worked really hard on putting together that first Kickstarter campaign, something I had always wanted to do, and launched it with as much terror as excitement. I decided to aim for about $6000, which was as much as I thought I could raise on the outside. The real cost of the project was at least $10,000 for the art alone, but I still had my job and it seemed like it would last long enough to cover the difference. The reality was that I wasn't even sure that I *should* continue.

I wanted to keep the story going, but were there enough people out there reading it to make it worthwhile? Running a Kickstarter would prove things one way or the other.

We had a party to celebrate the launch, and many of my coworkers, probably sick of hearing about it for so long, were generous enough to jump in for a copy of the book or some artwork. The hardcore fans jumped in after them. We raised over $2000 in the first few days and I cheered internally. Then the pledges slowed, they plateaued, and suddenly there was no more movement towards the final goal.

I flew to South Africa for a wedding and kept plugging away, trying to get to that final goal. I had a lot of great swag on offer, including leather-bound reproductions of the journal I would make myself for $600 each. The problem was, along with many of the other rewards I was offering, they would cost practically as much to produce as I would receive. Just printing and binding each journal cost something like $400. But I wasn't so worried about making money at that point. I just wanted to see if there was enough engagement to continue.

I should have worried more about making money, but we'll get to that later.

What concerned me most at the time was that perhaps I was wrong. Maybe the project wasn't so interesting, the writing not so great. Maybe I should quit. I mean it certainly was a crazy project and I knew it. Then suddenly, people bought a few more of those leather-bound journals, pushing me within striking distance of my goal, and all self-reflection went out the window.

BREWERY BACHELOR

My buddy Jeff was getting married. You might remember I mentioned my hetero-life-partner Jeff earlier; he was a friend in college, roommate after, and has been one of my most consistent supporters over the course of my floundering creative career. Between us, Jeff was the dead-set bachelor while I was always

wishing I could put single life behind me. So, it came as a surprise all around when he fell in love and decided to get hitched (while perhaps decreasingly a surprise that I was as single as ever).

I've always wanted to get married. It was something I figured I'd do straight out of college. I also grew up very religious, which is something I never talk about on my vlog because it doesn't really feel like the right space. One of the effects of this, however, was that I was very dedicated to the idea of saving myself for marriage.

This opens a door to a long conversation, but suffice it to say that I held to it with the same discipline I put behind a lot of goals in my life. Being pretty intense about whatever direction I choose, I decided I wouldn't even kiss anyone until I was engaged, maybe not until standing at the altar.

As you may have just said to yourself while reading, this was a terrible decision.

I had friends in college who managed to do this in one way or another and swore by it, but in retrospect, I don't know that I'd want to have my first kiss in front of my friends and family. I also no longer think it's healthy or natural. In fact, knowing myself, it seems grossly performative now. But I did think it was the right thing to do, for me, for way too long.

I ruined a lot of relationships along the way, including a few that I had while Jeff and I were in college. It turns out that most women do enjoy kissing. It also turns out that refusing to do so for an extended period of time puts a lot of unnecessary strain on pretty much any relationship, especially when the other party hasn't made the same decisions with her life.

I didn't have my first kiss until I was 26, on the ship in Togo. It was also about as far from the bright, romantic vision of the experience I had built up in my mind over those two and a half decades. I was burned out, depressed, and disillusioned.

When I finally kissed the woman I was dating, it was almost out of a sense of resignation. I was pretty terrible at it the first time, so at least I didn't find that out in front of my mom (there's always a silver lining to these stories). But I wasn't ready to go much further, and it turns out that women enjoy a lot of things beyond kissing as well. Holding out comes to feel like rejection, and that does not do wonders for long-term relationships.

I found myself in this very, very weird holding pattern. Wanting something I wouldn't let myself have and inflicting my confusion on any relationship into which I stumbled. This affected my relationship with Élodie, as you might expect, and then the women with whom I tried to rebound after. I just couldn't.

There was a lot of shame involved in these experiences for me. Shame because I was raised to believe that even wanting sex was shameful (until, magically, it was OK within the confines of marriage). Shame in being rejected along the way compounded by the shame of letting that desire show itself to someone else. Shame in doing the rejecting because I couldn't act on what I wanted, and now I'd brought that shameful desire out in someone else and hurt them in the process. *Vicious* doesn't begin to describe the cycle I made for myself.

I deleted the dating apps. I reinstalled them and failed to meet anyone and deleted them and reinstalled them. If I met someone who really seemed to like me, I shut down. If I got pushed away, I remained interested because it was safer to be interested in someone with whom there was no real possibility in the first place. When I got to Louisville, I was still reeling from how deeply I had fallen for Élodie. I was too emotionally immature to get past it the way I should have. I didn't stop reeling for years.

When Jeff told me he was getting married, I was happy for him and simultaneously sad. If nothing else, I consoled myself, at least Jeff and I would be bachelors together. We had always talked

about getting a loft Downtown Anywhere (something he and his wife are still open to because she's awesome—hi, Martha) and then we could just be that old-friend-duo that everyone wondered "Are they gay?" and we would just let them wonder because who gives a shit? We're just up here reading our newspapers, drinking coffee, and playing pétanque.

If Jeff was getting hitched while I was still floundering to figure out if I would ever have sex or not, I was really good and truly doomed to be alone forever.

Life on the road did not help with this at all. In fact, it compounded the problem. Ever since I was young, I had this fantasy whenever we went on road trips as a family that I was going to meet the girl of my dreams wherever it was we were going. She didn't seem to be in Pullman, but that didn't mean she wasn't hanging out on the beach at Lake Perrigin. This fantasy persisted until a few months ago.

Life on the road seemed romantic in its own ways, but it didn't take me places where I was likely to meet and click with someone. I wasn't even in the same place for more than a few days most of the time. Occasionally, my loneliness would become so tangible as a tension in my chest that I would feel compelled to turn to someone I knew and ask them out, regardless of any other factors. This usually happened at the worst possible moment, often with old acquaintances I simply hadn't seen in a year or two, and invariably collapsed in a cascade of awkward syllables.

I'm really good at taking rejection now. I'm thinking I could run a course on it for Skillshare if they ever want to follow through with that offer to sponsor my channel *cough cough*—but it took a long time to get over myself.

Ultimately, I didn't trust myself—because, I mean, just look at the emotional shitstorm raging inside me—but in a weird way I trusted them less. If a woman saw I was interested, she was

seeing something shameful in me. So, I hid how I felt.

In reality, it went beyond wanting to avoid rejection. I was a writer; I was very, very used to rejection. I was caught in an impossible catch-22—I had to find someone and build mutual interest without ever letting on I was interested. This led to a lot of attempts to skip all of the natural steps leading into a relationship, and as a result, a plethora of cringe-worthy moments ensued.

Strolling into Jeff's wedding weekend was rough not because I wasn't happy for him—I was (and remain so—Martha, again, you rule). It was rough because I was living in mobile isolation. I was lost. Even though I would often catch myself verbally externalizing this pain, literally saying "I don't want to be alone anymore" in private groans in hotels across the country, I didn't know what to do about it. Everything I tried failed to help.

If you get the sense that things were spinning out of control, we're on the same page.

We dressed up in ridiculous outfits and went on a brewery tour for Jeff's bachelor party. Hop in the back of an old Swiss army truck, jump out at the next brewery. There were some rowdier elements to the crew, but overall, it looked to be a tame event. We got a little drunker with each passing brewery and increasingly excited for the promised pizza finish at the end. It was reportedly Jeff's favorite spot in the area, and as we share an undying love for Pizza Pipeline, I knew that it would be a worthy crescendo.

Some of the aforementioned rowdy elements agitated for a strip club instead. Jeff's cousin Nolan and I pushed back that the bachelor had made it clear he wanted no such thing. Neither did we. Can you imagine me, after everything you just read, in a strip club? My head would implode.

We hopped into the army truck, bouncing around San Diego from brewery to brewery. We tried different beers, took a few tours, and things progressed about as you would expect.

Finally, the last stop of the night was upon us. I was famished, beyond ready for a pizza extravaganza. We came to a stop in a big parking lot, they popped the tailgate, and I hopped out with a grin. "Oh, yeah! Pizza ti—whatthef*ck?"

The rougher elements had bribed the driver. I was not going to get my pizza fix.

PHANTOMS OF THE UNREAL

What I was suffering while consulting, though I didn't really know it yet, was a steady loss of faith in myself.

I had always wanted to get back to Paris, but that desire began to wane along with everything else. It felt like everything good was receding slowly into a fog. I wanted to make movies out of the stories I was putting down as books, but that seemed increasingly out of reach. I thought I had something special to offer the world, ever since I was a kid. That light of belief in myself hadn't gone out, but it was being slowly smothered under deepening layers of doubt.

I hit some highs with Mercy Ships, despite the lows that came between them. I had been able to operate under extreme stress, in highly demanding jobs, with some incredible people from all over the world. We shared a purpose; we relied on one another. These brilliant and selfless people had seen something in me that they respected. Some had even gone so far as to love me. And many of the people we were there to help would have literally died without us.

Now, by comparison, I was working a joke of a job. The people I worked with were mostly concerned with earning as much money and hotel points as possible. The people we were there to help would rather we not. I lacked purpose. I certainly didn't feel like I was excelling at anything beyond bullshitting and juggling

expense reports. And even though I was doing all this to finance my dreams, those dreams only felt further and further away. Especially as *Into the Nanten* gained so little traction in spite of the late nights and financial strain.

Losing a relationship is always a challenge, one way or the other, but I never gave myself the proper time or space to really let go of Élodie. Even as she faded slowly, I didn't do the heavy lifting of shoving her the rest of the way out the proverbial door. She became my myth—the One That Got Away—and even though it was over, the phantom of her hovered over what I hoped could someday be.

I would pace my hotel rooms, agitated from a long day of work and an evening spent writing. What was this even worth? Maybe I should just give it all up and try to take a creative job.

But where could I go?

I couldn't just give up on this plan, on these sacrifices I had made. I was pot-committed. But I was so lonely. I physically ached from it. But where do you turn to fix that?

Trips to see friends were always good, but staying meant starting over. My family had reassembled in Spokane at this point. Seeing them was always good for me, but my sister was on her way to getting married and my friends had largely left. When I shared my struggles, most of the ones that remained tended towards inferring I should give up. The rest were kind but couldn't relate. It wasn't that I felt I didn't belong anymore; I didn't feel like I could belong anymore.

And so, I kept hopping on planes. Lying alone in hotel rooms. Thinking about phantoms and wishing I had someone real.

STATISTICALLY UNVIABLE IN LOVE

Online dating was a thing before I left for the ship but obviously not something you can put too much use when access to Facebook is questionable. Tinder wasn't even a thing until I'd been on the ship for almost two years.

As soon as Élodie and I came to our ignominious end, I hopped on all of them. I'd seen the end coming for some time, whether or not I was willing to admit it to myself. I just wanted to stem the flood of loneliness. I wanted to feel wanted—something that had eluded me for months, which, when you feel that way despite being in a relationship, is about the sharpest of feelings on the loneliness spectrum.

I could hear the digital sirens to my self-respect singing, and I veered off course to heed their call.

Over time, I had my fair share of bad dates. Through the variety of awkward and cringe-worthy moments, a defining feature was that they always felt like work.

What I know now is that this was largely because I wasn't ready to date at all. I needed to take time, root out some cancerous lies, and start loving myself the way I wanted to be loved. Jeff had been right. And rebounding was not going to help. Especially when I still wasn't willing or ready to go all the way with anyone.

I'd love to reach back across time and slap my former self, because this was only a recipe for making everything worse. Much worse.

The women I dated must have had quite the time of it. If they didn't really like me, I stuck around (safe). If they started to like me or, God forbid, like me a lot, I came up with some reason to bounce (danger zone). I was looking for something they couldn't give and offering what I couldn't either.

That's not to say that I was dating like a maniac. Dating apps, for a lot of men at least, are a quick lesson in statistical humbling if we're paying attention. At least it was for me (maybe it's only me?). For the uninitiated, Tinder's infamous mechanic is based on swiping left or right on profiles on your phone. Swipe left and you reject; swipe right and you hope they didn't reject you. If they also swipe right, you match, and a line of communication opens.

No one matched with me. I mean, technically not no one, but if we're talking percentages, it has to be below 1%. It got to the point that I made a really depressing game out of it, swiping right indiscriminately until I ran out of my swipe quota for the day. Zero matches. I'd wait and try again when my swipes reset, usually while traveling to Chicago or anywhere else that I was spending the weekend (you have to pay for unlimited swipes and I already felt depressed enough about the situation without paying for the gut punches). I swiped so fast, the names didn't even have time to load.

Zero matches. I had friends that didn't believe me, so I included them in the game by handing them my phone and letting

them do it for me. Even with their skilled swiping skills: zero matches.

I could hear the sirens over the crash of the waves around me, somewhere ahead, I swore, but I couldn't see them through the spray. Unfortunately, unlike Jason, I didn't have any Argonauts to tie me to the mast and keep me from veering ever closer towards the danger.

It's not a great feeling to think you're digitally unviable for love in an online era. Especially when you live alone and spend all of your time in airports and hotels. And then it gets weird:

I get flown to Des Moines for a couple of weeks of work and have equally bad luck. The irony was that a woman I work with, who I find wildly attractive, seems to be slowly coming around to finding me viable in a completely analog way. The problem is, as I quickly find out, that she's married. Very unhappily so. The siren song rises higher.

So, here I am, lying alone in a hotel room, dying for someone just to sit and have a meal with me at the P.F. Chang's down the street. As fate would have it, there's a perfectly willing candidate texting me. She's says she's Googling me, that she's found my books.

"I wish I was talented like you," she sends me. I shake my head against the enchantment and dodge the shale of innuendo, veering towards a clear path that looks like reassurance.

"I'm sure you're very talented in your own ways—you're great at keeping the doctors from going crazy on us."

"Well now that you mention it…I am really good at stripping…"

Rocks in the path ahead.

But not just the rocks of adultery. The press of the loneliness makes this feel inevitable, makes it a fight to dodge the

rocks themselves but also to keep from having the ship torn apart beneath me by raging waters and whatever monsters have followed me here.

I am still young, afraid to be direct for all my conviction to what I think is right. The apps aren't providing any alternatives. The siren's song shifts tone and I think perhaps I can get out of this by finding someone else. Someone unattached and desperate like me. I look to Craigslist "Seeking" ads and find myself casting lines in whatever direction seems remotely promising. I receive nothing in return.

I do, however, continue receiving texts. "I don't like being alone at home for the whole weekend…" I dig through want ads and weird websites I've never heard of before. "My husband left yesterday for a long business trip." I stumble across a website advertising dates 'for hire.' "I don't really feel safe here all by myself." I pick up the phone.

It's a stranger's number. I don't know this woman, her real name, or how her voice will sound. All I know is that I want someone to sit with me, have a nice meal. To feel wanted.

But as the rings sound and the song hits a tremulous pitch, lighting strikes and I see new rocks within the waves. I hang up the phone before she can answer. Deep breath. Walk it off. Just go eat and suck it up.

The sirens pass harmlessly off the starboard side, their rocks scraping at my ship but unable to puncture the hull. I go eat at P.F. Chang's alone. I wander into the mall and see a movie, get popcorn for two because somehow it's cheaper, and finish the entire thing alone. Then I sit in a photo booth, pick the cartoon PB&J couple's theme out of a sense of morbid irony, and take a few photos of myself, slumping deeper out of the frame with every shot, totally and completely alone.

DEATH OF A SELF-RIGHTEOUS PRICK

The bachelor party had hit its peak along with my hunger. I jumped out of the back of the Swiss army truck in what I thought was a pizza parlor's parking lot and was shocked to discover no such thing. I had never been to a strip club before. Truth be told, there was a small thrill that went through me at the taboo of it, but I immediately doused that thrill with cold holy water and demanded we go get pizza instead. I discovered I was about the only person who really wanted pizza at this point.

They sold pizza inside, I was told. I shuddered.

We filed inside and I felt increasingly uncomfortable at every turn. Were they going to post my image from their security footage online? Was the whole world going to find out I was in a seedy establishment of ill repute?

I distanced myself from the group immediately upon admission. I sidestepped through the tables with my hands up at my shoulders, half to prove they weren't touching anything and half to keep from being touched. I'd just gotten this ridiculous American-flag suit; I didn't want it stained by God-knew-what if I bumped a table. And considering everything was covered in velour...

I made for the bar. I needed a drink. The lights were low, the music high, and the bar sat empty at the opposite end of the room from the stage. The irony of strip clubs in some parts of the country, I quickly discovered, was that if you want to see boobs, they won't serve alcohol. No boobs? Beer's OK.

I huddled up on a stool with a Coke and did my best not to look at all the boobs in question as they passed me by. I was mortified. How the hell had I wound up there? I let pretty much everyone that tried to get my attention know that I wasn't like these

guys, I didn't normally do stuff like this. Rotate back to Coke. Ignore the world as it flashed by.

It's hard to ignore naked women for long, even for an expert on repression. One of the bartenders asked me what I was into, and I replied, "Intelligence," without realizing just how much of an ass I was being. She winked and a minute later, a woman hopped onto the stool next to me. She introduced herself like a normal person, despite being in her underwear, and struck up a conversation. It turned out she genuinely was intelligent, finishing up her master's and planning on getting a job teaching. She seemed cool. I was suspicious.

We talked for the next two hours, which, as it turned out, meant that she went two hours without getting paid. I started to open up. We talked about life and our dreams, where we'd been and where we wanted to go. She was real, and I started to feel ashamed of myself for thinking I was better than her (and everyone else in the place) when I walked in. That ache that had driven me to pace so many hotel rooms began to warm and then slowly untangle. I felt a connection.

Eventually, she had to work. I understood, though suddenly I didn't want her to go. One of the rougher elements had gotten kicked out pretty early on, I discovered, for trying to take photos, among other things. The rest of the crew were splitting up as the remaining rough elements wanted to ratchet things up another three levels and the other guys just wanted to go to bed. But not before springing a surprise on me.

Having seen my long-running conversation at the bar, they had become convinced I was destined to take this particular lady home with me at the end of the night. They grabbed me and brought me over to a chair on the side. Knowing that this was the first time I'd ever been in a place like this, one of them had

decided to buy me my first lap dance. I'm pretty sure it was done in a generous spirit, but my alarm bells began to flare.

It was the same woman with whom I'd just spent the last two hours talking. "Gotta compensate her for all that chitchat, at least," the guy said before leaving me on my own. She walked over, smiled, and told me the rules as she started dancing. Only light touching. Nothing more.

I sat on my hands.

But that wasn't what I really wanted to do. She seemed so perfect now that she was so close. So smooth, tiny goosebumps rippling across her waist. I looked up, past the rest of what could only be described as incredible, and saw a different face from before. A slanted mouth that mimicked her earlier smile. Distant eyes that no longer saw me as a new friend. Just another client.

I was inches away from a vision of what I wanted, and I couldn't have been further from it. I cracked a little on the inside as I watched her withdraw. Physically, she was right there in front of me, closer than she had been all night, but in reality, she may as well have been a thousand miles away. I offered to pay for another as my friends winked and left the club. I told myself it was because I owed her as much. In reality, I just wanted to be near someone beautiful for a few minutes. To pretend someone beautiful wanted to be near me. Not to lose a connection I'd already killed.

I gave her enough money for another dance and with it destroyed any of the good the previous two hours had done. I lost the confidence our conversation had given me, reduced to another schmuck in a club.

You can't buy love, you can't even rent it, and the simulation you receive in trying only broadens the emptiness you were trying to fill. My ship ground against the shale, a glancing blow as the wind and waves shoved it sideways and spinning out to sea. The

sirens were never themselves the danger, at least not in any external sense. They were something within me, steering rather than luring. This loneliness wasn't being inflicted upon me; I was doing it to myself.

BRING THE RIGHT DATE

This was a lot to handle. It should come as no surprise that I didn't manage to process it all on the spot, or even on the long Uber ride back to the bachelor pad alone. I'm still working through a lot of this today (hello, confirmed bachelorhood).

In the meantime, the wedding itself finally took place. The date I brought was a woman I met through the EMR consulting scene, someone else who had unlimited travel at her fingertips and a taste for adventure. She was energetic, fun, and quick on her feet. This came in handy, as every time I left her alone at the reception, she got hit on by one of the groomsmen from the night before.

I asked her how she was holding up and she said it was no problem. She could handle a little extra attention. Her way of handling it? By telling them fabricated, wildly licentious stories about either me, herself, or both. Apparently, she was a porn star in LA (untrue) who had met me on a trip to Jamaica (true) and who had fallen head-over-heels for me (questionable) because of how amazing I was in bed (obviously unproven at this point).

She was quite the wing-woman of a date.

If those guys' respect for me had risen after the strip club, they didn't know what to do with me after discovering that I had adult film stars falling for my prowess. My reputation was thoroughly and impressively inflated from that moment on.

As for my date, we had a good long conversation that evening about my hang-ups with pushing things to the point that she could genuinely vouch for said prowess. For any young gentlemen

reading this at home: it's not the most romantic conversation to have at a wedding. She made a persuasive argument that I was taking things too seriously and, possibly more importantly, making unilateral decisions that needed to be shared. I agreed that I was taking things too seriously, but I wasn't sure how to change course on that yet. As for decisions, how far I wanted to take things, that was definitely my call. I did decide, however, to take a risk when I walked her to her car, took her in my arms, and gave her a long kiss goodnight. She was happy with the compromise.

I was coming to realize my need to do so. I had mistaken the source of the danger in these exchanges, in seeking what I wanted in impossible places. If the sirens weren't something to be feared, or at least the source of my misguidance was generated within, then maybe it was best if I untied myself from the mast and got back to sailing the ship.

CHAPTER SEVEN:

BOOMERANG

ONCE A NERD

I always dreamed of founding my own tech company—at least, I have since it became a trendy thing in college. I watched as Apple, Facebook, Google, and the rest fed into the mythos of changing the world through creative technological solutions. I wasn't an engineer or programmer, but that didn't keep my imagination from being captured. Besides, life is too short not to explore everything that interests you. Ideally, you can jump on it right when the mood strikes and your momentum is building.

Most of the time, my drive to learn is spurred by a specific project or thing I want to create. While I can focus on one such thing until completion, I'm interested in too many to specialize. It's why I love the alleged full quote: "A jack of all trades is a master of none, but oftentimes better than a master of one."

Whether or not it's true, it certainly helps me feel better than if I was supposed to have a specialty by now.

I've always written stories. I wrote and produced my first play in the first grade. There's a recording of it around here somewhere—I'll find it and make a vlog about it sometime. I made my first movie in the fourth grade, *Jason and the Argonauts*—also worthy of inclusion if I can find it. I never stopped. But I also really enjoyed diving into computers, which were thankfully ubiquitous in my community (back before they were just ubiquitous).

My dad made it a point to get one as soon as it was remotely affordable, an IBM x486 desktop machine cast in the most offensive inoffensive beige you can imagine. We took turns and, since we couldn't afford any games, spent a lot of time pretending we were amused by Notepad, Paint, and whatever else was around (thankfully, eventually, *Carmen Sandiego* and *Number Crunchers* would grace us with their educational glory).

But I was also fascinated with websites, a growing

phenomenon that we discovered as we slowly embarked on adventures beyond the AOL welcome screen and into ICQ chatrooms. My buddy Ben turned me on to HTML and CSS in high school and got me hooked on writing simple web pages from scratch. There was something magical about telling a computer what you wanted to see and then bringing that vision to life on the screen. I enrolled in an extracurricular hardware course with Ben, but getting up early to get certified on computer innards was pushing it for me. I let him handle the deep tech.

This preference for using computers over building them persists to this day. The possibilities of what you could create seemed endless, and I would try my hand at plenty. I even started building my own Flash video player from scratch. Not the best use of my time, but it was a noble failure.

I skipped the first year of multimedia courses in high school, which focused on Photoshop, so I could dive straight into video courses. My teacher agreed on the condition that I didn't bother him with stuff I should have learned in that first year. I made it my goal to be no burden. I would become a thorn in his side for totally different reasons.

I dove deeper into making videos with every opportunity, steadily dropping out of sports and spending more and more time editing. In retrospect, this might have been a good sign that I was more introverted than anyone realized at the time.

SOMETHING HAS TO CHANGE

My return to the Shores of the Known, in the hopes of resupplying and launching back out to sea, took its toll in unexpected ways. I was getting too much alone time in Springfield, regardless of how introverted I may have become. I'm definitely an extrovert with introverted work tendencies, or maybe an

extroverted introvert. . . We can get into my psychological profile in another book. In this book, in Springfield, I was careening towards a fresh kind of trouble: I have never been so angry in my life.

Have you ever pulled up to a stoplight, bobbing your head to the rhythm of one of your favorite tunes? *Tap tap tappity tap*, go your hands on the steering wheel. You smile to yourself, just a little, because in that moment, life is good. You glance over to your left at the car next to you, where the driver is also tapping their steering wheel.

Except they're tapping it so hard, it looks more like they're playing Whac-A-Mole. And they're shouting. It doesn't really matter if it's at anyone in particular, because they caught you looking at them and things just got awkward. Your smile pulls down on one side as your eyebrows go askew. You return your gaze to the road ahead and pull forward on green, thinking, *What a weirdo. Thank God I'm not that guy.* Well, dear reader, that weirdo was me.

As I drove through town, or south to the St. Louis airport, or north for a weekend in Chicago, I would scream at the world. Mostly at Springfield. I hated the city, my job, and increasingly my life.

So much of it seemed to come from nowhere. For starters, with the exception of frustrated moments spent impeded by malfunctioning technology, I wouldn't describe myself as an angry person. As for the rest, there wasn't anything overtly wrong with me, my job, or my life. I was getting lots of exercise, making decent money, and traveling the country more than I ever had before. And yet, there was a storm broiling just beneath the surface that I couldn't get a handle on.

I'd gotten tastes of this in Louisville and through my bouncing around the Midwest, but I think the ever-changing scenery kept me more in the sad-and-docile loneliness camp. Back then, there was a lot of time spent staring blankly at new highways.

The crush of night forcing my vision into a tunnel whose only light came not at the end but from the quick flashes of dashed paint below.

Springfield lasted long enough to become familiarity, and there's something about familiarity with the mundane that breeds contempt. Not to harsh too heavily on Springfield; the majority of the people we interacted with were kind. The nurses I wound up spending the majority of my time with were fun. But the repetition of showing up to work only to wait for work to materialize steadily ground me down.

This anger served as fuel for my first successful attempt at dieting. I would get up, grab the egg white wrap at Starbucks (the lowest calorie count on the menu at the time), and head to the windowless box or the basement of a clinic for the day to sit until it was time for a snack. Then I'd walk to the nearest grocery store, grab some fruit, and return to whatever chair I had been warming all morning.

We'd leave for lunch, I'd have a salad, and we'd return to warm our chairs. Our time in clinical purgatory would eventually come to its close for the day and I would head straight to the gym, change, lift for forty-five minutes, go run 10k, and finish out with a protein shake. I'd head back to my hotel, work on *Into the Nanten*, eat an open-faced Jimmy John's sub, and do the whole thing over again the next day.

I lost forty pounds. My soul was mixed in there somewhere, but I guess it was dead weight anyway.

FROM JUNGLE TO JUNGLE

Into the Nanten, in case you were wondering where *that* thread left off, was a success on Kickstarter and the first early signs that perhaps this return to shore might pay off down the road. We

crossed the line with a few days to spare, and I breathed a sigh of relief. I really wanted to keep the story going and it felt validating to know that there were at least a hundred people willing to pay to see it continue. I didn't let the fact that the campaign basically made no money get me down—I still had a job, right?

The reason it made so little money was twofold—the overall cost of the project being much higher than what I had set as a campaign goal, and that of the rewards themselves. I made a lot of little rewards and a handful of big ones, the smallest of which was a handwritten note from the protagonist of the story. It was a copy of what he had written to his mysterious friend and then smuggled out of prison. I printed off over a hundred of them, hand-tore the edges to make them look more like parchment, and then crumpled them up once, twice, and then a third time before rolling them into tight little sticks of secrecy and mailing them to backers. It took hours of crumpling paper in both hands—I got cramps. It was awesome.

On the other extreme, I made leather-bound journals with fully redesigned interiors including mud and blood spatters, as well as printed art of various sizes. Everything shipped on time. I was really proud of what we created. And then I dove straight into season two.

This time, to make things even more immersive, I hired a voice actor to produce each entry as a podcast episode that could be released in real time with the entries as they came out. It was also awesome. Dennis, the actor in question, brought another dimension of vibrancy to the project.

I figured we were on our way to something big. Something that would really move. And, if it did, perhaps I could finally cast off to sea, making the transition into writing full-time and creating the fiction of my dreams as my main focus.

But the financial realities were increasingly evident. Even as I flew around the country attending conventions and hawking my wares, and even as my books and the concept itself sold really well one-on-one, there wasn't enough momentum building. The books themselves were expensive—it turns out that printing a full-color paperback leaves little margin for profit—and there wasn't enough volume to make up for it. If I wanted to keep producing *Into the Nanten* and grow beyond it, I was going to need to find a way to make some real money.

And then my buddy Brian called with an interesting idea.

SPAGHETTI FOR SPRINGFIELD

Back when my coworkers and I still tried to take lunch together, before we realized we really didn't have a lot in culinary common, we tried this Italian joint. I didn't realize until just now that I never went back. It was standard mediocre Springfield fare, but in an environment that leaned even harder than usual into the "I'm a retired Abraham Lincoln impersonator and even I think this is schwanky!" department.

Brian called about the same moment that I placed my order. The more uptight selection of my coworkers were annoyed with me for disappearing through most of lunch. I had good reason, however, because the phone call was set to change my life.

That, and talking to Brian was more fun. Whenever Brian and I get on the phone, we invariably chat for an hour minimum, regardless of how quick a call we swear it's going to be. Blame for this shifts regularly enough that I think we can just own it as something we do to ourselves. I stepped back outside into the crisp cold of the Illinois winter.

I've known Brian literally as long as I've known anyone from my time with Mercy Ships. I met him back when I was just starting the process on my first exploratory trip down to the headquarters in Texas. Brian and I wound up working together in

the IT department and became great friends, eventually traveling to over a dozen countries together (he has the official count in a spreadsheet somewhere—I think he also influenced my love of good spreadsheets). I have a lot of stories about Brian, but on this particular call, he wanted to know how much it would cost for me to build a website and possibly a Kickstarter campaign for him.

He and a couple of friends were looking to build a Bluetooth bracelet for kids, named Boomerang, which could be worn when out and about and alert parents when the attached child got too far away for comfort. The team he'd assembled included people with whom he had already built robots for everything from NASA competitions to the *BattleBots* TV show.

I was intrigued. I had always wanted to be a part of a team like this, and more importantly, I got the feeling that they needed someone around who *wasn't* an engineer. I asked if they'd be interested in bringing me on as a co-founder rather than paying me for my services.

This intrigued Brian. When Brian gets intrigued, it's usually a sign that something is either very right with an idea or very, very wrong. I remember pacing the sidewalk outside that cheesy Italian joint, salt crackling under my wingtips as I silently questioned the wisdom of diving into yet another massive project. Brian said he'd get back to me.

I went back inside to my irritated coworkers and took my lukewarm pasta to go.

MOMENTUM IN MINNEAPOLIS

Throughout my time consulting, I attended as many sci-fi/fantasy conventions as I could manage in hopes of furthering my fledgling career (and pumping *Into the Nanten* while it was running). What I loved most about the convention scene was meeting other

writers, people whose careers were much further along than my own, and feeling included by them in the midst of the festivities.

There were a number of them for whom it didn't matter that I was some upstart self-publishing nerd flying in from an obscure job site in the Midwest. They just wanted to drink and talk shop. This is where I learned about Bar Con—when everyone convenes for the real socializing after hours—and the strategy for "Bar Conning It"—Gail Carriger showed up at Bar Con for a convention she wasn't officially attending which, she told me, was the best part and came without the entrance fees.

After writing my first four books in total isolation (it's harder to get much further removed from the SF/F community than a port in Freetown, Sierra Leone), this new scene was a breath of fresh air. I reveled in it, doing my best to put myself in the path of the most potential friendships possible.

Writers are weird. Most of us know this already, but what doesn't register for many is how painfully accessible they are to their communities. Actors, musicians, and athletes generally don't congregate in the hotel bar when the hotel is chock full of nothing but fans. Where those public figures tend to have agents, managers, and a variety of other buffers between them and their public, the average published author will actually shake your hand if you take a moment to reach for it. This is both amazing and terrible all at once.

The amazing part is how you can very quickly attach yourself to a group of new people, make friends, and discover that they're all incredibly talented individuals along the way. Much like travel, conventions are environments that engender a sense of curiosity and a willingness to chat that don't usually exist within many writers (they prefer to hide away alone and write for a reason). While the bigger names among them might be a little wary of newcomers, and the very biggest names unfortunately have to

hide with the athletes and movie stars, the majority are readily available and looking to mingle. This makes for some really fun conversations—especially for a fresh-out-of-isolation baby writer like me.

You are still, however, encouraged to have some sense of situational awareness and at least a base level of social aptitude. This brings us to what a few of us came to refer to as Writing Desk Moments.

Worldcon, my very first SF/F convention, was a very steep learning curve. Thankfully, I managed to fumble my way into some fantastic friendships that I hope I maintain for the rest of my life. I also found myself on the receiving end of some awkward situations that, I quickly came to realize, plague authors and public figures of all kinds.

I was working a booth I had secured for my very first convention, a total newbie to the scene, hoping that no one would call me out for the impostor I was. I had paid a solid chunk of money to hang art in the show and deck out said booth, let alone pay the rent necessary to use it. I printed books and art to sell, all hoping to point people towards *Into the Nanten* and build momentum for the upcoming second season. I took time off work, got up early, worked late, and socialized like crazy whenever I wasn't hawking books. I may have been a newb, but I was a pro.

Up comes a guy who sees a stationary target. He's got his own book, you see; he's been working on it for some time. He'd like to tell you about it. He seems oblivious to the fact that you're standing behind a table you paid for, covered in goods you've created to sell. He just seems to think you'd be more interested in hearing about his idea for a new manuscript than talking with potential readers. He asks no questions. Offers little preamble. He simply talks at you.

The inverted version of this that was slightly more endearing but still registered on Fraut's Scale of Frustration was

the people who would shuffle up just long enough to hand you their business card with their author website printed on it before scurrying away.

Here's the harsh reality for all involved: I don't want to read your book, dude. I'm here to sell mine.

The very pinnacle of this was a guy who was carrying around his own modular writing desk. Yes, you read that correctly. He was carrying around a very small writing desk. He walked up to my booth and started telling me about how, with this box strapped around his chest, he could in fact write anywhere. How there were tiny drawers in it that he could fill not only with pens and paper, nay, he could also fill them with his *ideas*.

He was a wandering bard, an itinerant monk of the cult of story, and hidden with this box he had crafted many moons prior, he could weave a tale of such gravitas and import that yaaaaarrrrrrrghhhhhh!

This guy happened to strike at the same moment that my new artist-acquaintance John Picacio was being assailed by a particularly sticky Painter of his own. Ten minutes in and we managed to make eye contact. A subtle wink was shared.

I edged out from behind my booth, nodding in feigned interest as the Bard continued to perform his monotone ballad. John made a similar maneuver, beguiling his Painter from his inert state into motion. We slowly spun our victims closer, maintaining just enough eye contact to indicate we were still listening. As much as we had wished them gone moments prior, they couldn't be permitted to part from us now. Not yet.

We met in the middle of the artist alley. John and I shook hands, surprised by this chance meeting. And oh, has your Painter met my Bard? How much they must have in common! Together, they would be capable of such brilliance.

We turned them to each other, the fateful introduction made, and set them spinning off on their own. A whirlwind of words and lofty ambitions once again set loose on the world but, for once, conjoined with an elemental force of equal measure. Their lonely journey had come to its finale, each talking happily at the other and never taking in a word. John and I sighed, smiled, and returned to our work.

I like to think that those two made great friends and eventually did go on to create something magnificent for the world to enjoy. I'd hate for so much hot air to go to waste.

YOU'VE GOTTA LEAP SOMETIME

The second season of *Into the Nanten* launched online, one entry at a time. I wrote on the road, listened to the audio recordings in laundromats, and managed the art from wherever I had cell reception. Boomerang meetings happened with increasing frequency as well. As the circuit design progressed and challenges were ironed out, we got more serious.

I was working on losing a swordsman deeper in a jungle of my own creation while also conceptualizing a bracelet to keep real kids from getting lost at all. Both fronts advanced slowly as I drove around Springfield screaming at their horribly timed stoplights and wishing I were anywhere else in the world.

I wanted to write full-time. I wanted to travel for my writing rather than for someone else's business. For my stories to be so well loved that these conventions would be about meeting fans rather than trying to find and make them. I wanted to invest more in the art that supported it, to make my world even bigger and more immersive. I wanted to create a universe, fill it with gripping stories, and share them with everyone around me.

I knew that if I wanted to break into this dream life I kept

imagining, I'd have to take a big risk at some point. I figured now was a better time than ever to take a leap. It meant sticking to shore for longer, extending my resupply time rather than spending it at sea in pursuit of that life. Any time beyond what was necessary on the Shores of the Known threatened to drive me to despair. But the opportunities just a little further down the coast also offered the chance for better supplies if any one of them worked out, perhaps a better ship. It seemed well worth taking the risk.

One of the publishers I had met along the way had told me that they were open to me if I ever wanted to submit work. We talked about what books I might write next, and they said that of all the ideas I had banging around, the post-apocalyptic would probably do best. While I had always wanted to find a way to remain independent, having a traditionally published book or two seemed like a great way to find some new fans and add legitimacy to my name.

Publishing, as a rule, is a poor man's game. The margins on paper are pretty thin to begin with, and most books don't sell many copies. Everyone has a pipe dream of becoming a bestseller—I'd be willing to bet my lunch that you yourself have dreamed of being a bestselling author at least once in your life. Let me make a quick aside here to give you a sense of how good a chance any given book has to sell well.

Walk into a bookstore of your choosing, let's say a nice big Barnes & Noble (assuming they're still with us by the time this is in your hands). Ignore the displays; those are outliers. Walk two rows deep, hang a right, and make your way down past three sets of shelves. Now stop, look to your left. Not at eye level. Look down near your feet. You see that book, the one that only has one copy with its spine showing between the spines of seven other books that also only have one copy on offer with only their spines showing? How many copies of that book do you imagine are selling?

In many arenas of publishing, selling 500 books is pretty good. 1,000 is solid. If you sell 5,000, you're doing great. You could even be hitting a bestsellers list, depending on the week.

If your cut is 17%, you might be bringing home a couple of bucks a book if you're lucky—which means you'd be lucky to clear $10,000 in royalties. But that doesn't mean you make $10,000 in royalties; your book sales have to earn out the advance first, which is an achievement in itself. By the time many authors clear that mark, their book has been discounted so significantly, they're now making pennies per sale.

So, you can see that publishing isn't usually a road to riches (or fame, but we can talk about that another time). It is, however, a road to legitimacy. There are doors that won't open for an author until they have a book on the shelves, regardless of whether it's on display or shoved in a dark corner somewhere. A broader range of people will think of you as a "real" author. Reviewers are more likely to pick up and review your book. Conventions are more likely to accept your pitch for panels. Business life, in a phrase, gets a little easier.

That's not to say it's easy—publishing is still a brutal industry with little room for error and less for genuine screw-ups. But as it's an industry built on longstanding traditional gateways, your path smooths out with every gatekeeper who lets you pass.

I had long resisted the urge to pass through any of these gates. My ambitions for my fiction are too big for traditional publishing—I simply want to do too much and I want to go too big. But that doesn't mean that having a little blue checkmark next to my name wouldn't help a little in accomplishing those dreams.

So, I set out to write a post-apocalyptic book that had been banging around in my head for some time. The only mistake was that it wasn't the book I wanted to write.

FULL THROTTLE

I tend to take things to extremes. Not in every arena, but where my goals and dreams are concerned, I've steadily removed layers of inhibition over time.

When the time finally came to leave Springfield, things were looking pretty dire on the EMR landscape. The major transitions had taken place and the need for consultants had all but dried up. Most of my colleagues were looking to pick up full-time jobs at hospitals and clinics as close to home as possible. The switch to stability meant no more travel and lower pay, which basically were the only two things that had kept me from running screaming into the woods while doing the job. As the end drew nigh, the woods looked all the more tempting.

Into the Nanten was off and running, the audience for it growing (as far as we could tell) even if it wasn't massive. Boomerang discussions and calls were becoming increasingly time-consuming. I had to start working on developing the logo, messaging, packaging, and upcoming Kickstarter campaign— basically everything outside the technical realm. And I was really enjoying the process.

Even though I sat silent through the majority of each of our team calls, I loved learning about the ins and outs of the device. I felt especially satisfied on the occasions where I was able to chip in with a helpful observation or two. This was another group of people operating at high levels in their given fields—another group whose respect I found deep satisfaction in earning.

Things were picking up speed. I had some money stashed in my savings. It was now or never.

My parents had moved back up to Washington State, settling in Spokane, where they had friends and my sister was living with her new husband. My mom had a pretty wild brain surgery

lined up (they were going to implant actual electrodes in her brain!) and I figured it was a good time to head back and stay with them. I could be available to help as they needed it while simultaneously trying to get my new independent life off the ground.

I had a book I was prepping to send to a publisher. I had a third season of *Into the Nanten to Kickstart*. And I had a tech company I was getting ready to launch. Even if one or two of these things failed, one of them had to come through and pay the bills, if not put me firmly on the map.

It was time to take a massive leap and catch a breeze in my parachute. Or at least hope I caught a solid branch on the way down.

Chapter Eight:

Temperate Dives Turn to Tropical Faceplants

YE BE HERE

BEWARE

TREASURE MAPS ARE LIES!

LIVING WITH THE RENTS

I'm not going to say that I was thrilled to move back in with my parents, regardless of how much strategic sense it might have made (or however I sold it to myself to make it palatable).

Don't get me wrong; my parents are fantastic. I'm still very grateful to this day that I was able to move in with them. There was a bed of my own and an endless supply of PB&J sandwiches, not to mention nacho fixings for evening snacks, so, for all intents and purposes, I was a kept man.

But as an adult male of Puritanical American roots, this was the exact opposite direction from where life was supposed

to go. I was supposed to have my own farm by now, with a nice little woodshop, some chickens, maybe an ox or two if I played my capitalism right. Coming from a line of cowboys, firefighters, mechanics, and agricultural academics, moving back in with the rents was about as far from manhood as anything I'd been taught growing up.

Still, I wasn't too shaken by the looming threat of total emasculation—I was doing it for good reason and with a plan in hand. If things went well, I'd be out of there in no time and maybe even on my way back to Paris. I think this is what made it easy for my folks to take me in as well. They knew it would be temporary. I mean, we hoped it would be temporary. I mean. . .it was temporary, right? I keep pinching myself over this (can you imagine waking up and discovering the last three years had been a dream?! I'd die).

My heart was not light going into this, but I was hopeful. Hopeful that I could drag myself out of the state of perpetual frustration into which I had fallen. That for once, I might even succeed at something I set out to do. Categorically, I'm not the kind to keep one eye on the wake behind as I test out a new potential heading of my own. I dive in and don't look back.

I made a "temporary" office for myself at one of the local coffee shops, Coeur (coincidentally French for *heart*). With its high windows, walls lined with bright artwork, and tall square tables bathed in all this light, it was the perfect environment in which to write or work with a small team. I got to work in earnest.

My days were spent hammering out as many words as possible on a book I tentatively named *Couriers: OFF GRID* while still writing the end of *Into the Nanten*'s second season, publishing it daily, and coordinating the art and podcast. I frequently pivoted from fiction to phone calls and branding work for Boomerang. There was a lot of strategy to think through, structure to create, and assets to build.

At one point, Brian and I were clocking over thirty hours a week on phone calls between ourselves alone. I was still building random websites along the way to earn some extra cash, and prepping to launch the Kickstarter that would get us into a third season of *Into the Nanten*.

I was exhausted but exhilarated. My three projects, *Couriers*, *Into the Nanten*, and Boomerang, were newly discovered islands on the horizon, each promising riches enough to continue my voyage further into the Sea of the Unknown.

But in my determination to set sail, I had ignored the storm clouds forming on the horizon. My debts were growing in force, and instead of storm-proofing my little vessel, I was hemorrhaging what little cash I had left. If none of these islands gave up their treasure, I would be in the deepest financial hole of my life and very quickly forced to return to shore and resupply yet again. Assuming the ensuing shipwreck didn't take me with it.

TEMPESTS OF CREDIT

Spokane, as you may recall, hadn't been very good to me on the first go around. If there's a place that comes to mind when I think of "the Shores of the Known," it's pretty high on the list. That's not to say there aren't good things or good people in Spokane—I prefer it to a lot of places I've been, and Jeff and I would both insist that Pizza Pipeline is worth pulling off I-90 for lunch—but on a spiritual level, we don't gel.

Moving back to Spokane, into my parents' house of all places, would have been soul-crushing had it not been for Boomerang and *Into the Nanten*. In a way, I was making contact with the shore long enough to resupply for my daring attempt at relaunching into the Sea of the Unknown. All this while, the storm clouds that had been swelling overhead were reaching their breaking point.

At the same time that I was hammering away at building a tech company and writing two books, those clouds began to pour. Keeping your footing is a challenge when attempting to carry supplies across any beach. Add the gushing waters of financial instability and you're really asking for trouble. My credit card debt had grown substantially while consulting. It was surprisingly easy and very slow but steady.

There are two forms of getting paid to travel. One is when the company you work for buys your plane tickets, reserves your hotels, and gives you a company card for any expenses like gas or food while you're on the job. The other is when the client reimburses you after the fact. The pros of the first are that you don't have to worry about anything, it's taken care of, and your personal credit remains untouched (and often un-maxed). The cons are that you miss out on the almighty points and airline miles you would get if you used your own cards.

I existed in the world of the latter, where everything went on my own credit card and I filled out expense reports every week to get reimbursed. We were pressured to get as much credit as possible before going on the job to ensure we never found ourselves unable to buy multiple weeks' worth of airline tickets in advance (or you risked either overcharging the client for airfare or simply being unable to show up, which obviously made you look bad and at worst could get you fired).

The trick was that you often only got reimbursed for the travel you'd completed, not for anything you'd purchased in advance. So, suddenly, you had thousands of dollars of expenses sitting on your credit cards, waiting to get reimbursed weeks or months later.

Complicated as this was, it should have been simple enough to track in practice with good bookkeeping and some discipline. Even just working on projects short-term would have

curbed the dangers of the job. Unfortunately, my weakness in all things accounting, combined with a general sense of exhaustion and the thrill of making more money than I ever had, left me very vulnerable over time. All of the back-and-forth, the uncertainty over what was getting paid back when, and the need to keep pushing my credit limit higher for fear of finding myself stranded somewhere in northern Minnesota (hello, Canada!) made a mess. I made a mess.

It was easy to convince myself I was living within my means. I wasn't buying much, and I spent my weekends on friends' couches across the country with airfare I didn't have to pay for. But I was spending untold amounts on my own projects, like *Into the Nanten*, and very clearly finding ways to nickel-and-dime myself deeper into debt.

When the time came to make my initial investment of $5,000 into WearsIt, the company we founded to build Boomerang, I had to take out a loan to cover half of it. I couldn't back away from it then, I'd already invested hundreds of hours into the project, and I justified it by taking out a big-enough loan to consolidate some of my credit card debt at a lower interest rate. But I also needed that bigger loan to keep paying my bills, almost all of which was debt by this point.

You can see what kind of tornado I was stepping into, and you don't even have the financial figures in front of you.

Borrowing money to pay back money you've borrowed lends you some relief in that moment where you get to wash your hands of one of your long-term creditors.

"Huzzah!" you say to yourself. "I'm free!" Only to turn around and discover another creditor looming overhead, larger and somehow more implacable than the last.

This isn't a book on financial advice, and I'm obviously not qualified to give any, but I will say that I do not endorse this

method of personal finance. I know I'm not the only American who's applied it.

I burned through my savings and borrowed far more than I should have been allowed (and was offered plenty more opportunities to borrow even more), but I knew that my saving grace was just around the corner. It was the beginning of 2016, and all I needed was to survive long enough to launch my Kickstarter for *Into the Nanten*.

BETTER THAN YOU THINK

My first ITN Kickstarter, for season two of *Into the Nanten*, was successful by the skin of some really small teeth. I was in South Africa for a wedding during the campaign's middle-to-late-stages, which, if you're familiar with Kickstarter campaigns, are the painfully slow periods. And I was still underfunded. Then suddenly, before leaving my hotel for a hike with some friends, the alert came through that someone had bought the top tiered reward, putting us well within striking distance.

It was a $600 leather-bound journal, a handmade reproduction of the journal from the story, and *someone actually bought it*. I was ecstatic, leaping from cloud to cloud. And then someone ELSE bought one, and in no time, we were over our goal. I left my hotel room on a dizzy high to climb Table Mountain. The elevation we gained that day was nothing compared what I got from the knowledge that *Into the Nanten* would continue. I spun in circles at the summit, arms above my head in celebration. I was on top of the world, literally and figuratively.

Fast-forward to setting up my second ITN Kickstarter, for season three, and I was hoping for a similar miracle. More than that, I was hoping that the preceding year had grown our audience to a place where I wouldn't just cover the art and audio expenses

but that I might actually make money. Kickstarter is a funny thing as well because the sum total is counted as income, so I had to factor my own personal taxes into a sum of money that I might never personally touch. We can leave the painful ironies of the US tax code for that book I'll never write on financial advice.

ANYWAY—where the goal in the first Kickstarter was set by how much I reasonably thought we could raise from our existing readership, the goal in the second was set by actual cost.

"Why?" you might be asking if you skipped straight to this chapter for some reason. Because I had lost my job and was already overextending myself financially in just about every way I could manage.

I asked for the full amount: $15,000. $10,000 for art, $3000 for audio, and $2000 for fees and taxes (which was insufficient but I was nervous to ask for any more). I didn't know if we could do it or not, but I was hopeful. I had spent the previous two years traveling the country to promote the story, made contacts of all varieties within publishing, gotten on various podcasts, and on and on. The hype was up, the blurbs were in. This was going to be a big one, win or lose.

TAIPEI OR TAICHUNG?

To set the stage of this glorious publishing win, I received one of the few emotional boosts of my time in Spokane from Coeur, my coffeeshop-turned-office. They swapped the art out on their big gallery-sized walls once every six months, and I pitched them the idea of hanging art from my books.

I had some pieces left from showing in the gallery at Worldcon a year prior and was more than happy to print off a bunch more. Partially because I loved the idea of sharing my work with the community, and partially in hopes that it would sell. The

art was bright, vibrant, and colorful. They were all for it.

If you haven't seen Nimit Malavia's artwork from *Into the Nanten*, you really should do yourself a favor and just go stare at it for a while. It's magnificent. I measured and sketched up the walls in my notebook, designed how I wanted to show the art, created a few new compilations, and got to work. I think I dropped something like $1,200 on printing and mounting, but I only needed to sell a third of the art to make that back. And besides, it looked EPIC when it was finished.

The thing was that I needed to get it up in January, at the same time Brian and I were flying to Taiwan to look into manufacturing partners for Boomerang. As things came together and the printing process dragged on, it became clear that I would be receiving it on the same day I took off.

I've pulled a few extreme travel days, but this one hits a few unique categories. For one, I had met someone and asked her on a date that week. The problem was that my time was increasingly scarce, and so, thinking it would be fun to do an activity together, I asked her if she wanted to join us for hanging the art. I figured it would only take a couple of hours and then we could go grab dinner.

Random mid-book dating advice: activities yes, work-related activities no.

I also didn't end up receiving the artwork until later in the afternoon than anticipated. Thankfully, I had some friends willing to help for a few hours (some for even longer, thank you, Danielle), but it was a lot more than a couple of hours of work. I had something like nine walls over two rooms to fill up with a couple dozen pieces of art, all with Command strips which, while miraculous, are not quick to deploy. Especially when they pull off chunks of the wall next to hot water pipes (whoops).

It took me a solid six hours.

Somewhere in there, my date left. I can't blame her.

Now, the thing about hanging art before catching an international red-eye flight is that you arrive not only muscle-sore at the airport but with a wicked head start on the travel funk, as you've been sweating all day. Thankfully, with help from family and friends, I was able to get the art hung, my discontented date home (yep, wound up asking a friend to drive her home), and myself to the airport with just enough time to sprint through security and dive onto the plane. Scramble city. But the art was up and my books lined the mantel above the old fireplace. It looked great.

Brian and I met up in San Francisco and he got to play witness to the weird world of flying as a member of the highest possible class of airline loyalty status. A status I miss to this day, but one I'm happy not to deserve anymore.

Taiwan was a blast—I'd never been anywhere east of the Addis Ababa airport in Ethiopia. The usual elements you appreciate while traveling to a new place were delightful, between the food, architecture, and general vibe; I would love to go back. But touring manufacturing plants and having lengthy discussions with specialists whom we hoped to employ was even more fun. It felt so real—like what we were working on had legs. Like our future was just around the corner.

I played around with a new style of vlogging on this trip, inspired heavily by Casey Neistat's explosive new daily vlog, and had even more fun documenting the trip. My momentum was restored for the return to Spokane, and we doubled down on our efforts with Boomerang.

With this new boost of enthusiasm, I knew I only needed to buy myself some more time. If I could survive until the summer, with tentative plans to launch Boomerang by June or July, it would all be worth the risk. A successful Kickstarter for *Into the Nanten*, if it could pull in enough money to actually pay me something, would do just the trick.

THE FIRST JUMP OF MANY

I used to have a recurring dream where the dawning realization that I *could* fly was inversely correlated with my ability *to* fly. That is to say that as soon as I figured out, "Hey, I can fly!" I found myself grounded. Then I would spend the rest of the dream trying to fly, running and jumping, only to land flat on my feet like a normal schlub.

This sums up a lot of my waking life as well.

The trip to Taiwan reminded me that I was capable of flying. That my skills and experience made me a valuable asset to a high-level team of engineers and designers. That I could adapt quickly to foreign environments and adjust those skills to be viable within wildly new contexts. I was no impostor.

It inoculated me against the frustration of being grounded again in Spokane. Of being looked at sideways for even wanting to leave, let alone build a tech company or tell ridiculous fantasy stories. I narrowed my focus and pressed on with the work, counting on the gratification that would come from my eventual vindication. Those three islands ahead promised to provide it as I cast off, three places where treasure was rumored to be buried. I only needed one of them to come through.

And the first island offering that vindication was *Into the Nanten*.

The second season was nearing its close, the perfect time to launch a Kickstarter for the third season. We could get the art and audio underway early, and I would have money on hand to survive for another few months until Boomerang launched. I didn't expect Boomerang to make us rich anytime soon, but I was banking on it to survive until we turned that corner.

With the art on the walls and the support of the staff, Coeur was the perfect place to hold a launch party. We had live music, snacks, and plenty of computers and tablets available for

people to pledge their support as soon as we hit the button. It was a really fun night.

We hit our first thousand dollars that night during the soft launch, and then the next day, when I released it to the fans, we surpassed $3000. One-fifth raised in the first two days! It wasn't the overwhelming turn I was hoping for, but it was a solid start. I felt pretty good about things.

Usually, raising the first third within the first week is a good sign of health. We didn't hit the first third until the campaign's last week. The graph flatlined early and barely rose from there.

It didn't take that long for me to realize we weren't going to make it. No matter how quickly we dug for that buried treasure, it only seemed to sink deeper into the sand. *Into the Nanten* was about to come to a premature close. I could feel the ground reaching up and grabbing my legs.

There was no help on the way, no cavalry coming to save me or even give me a moment's reprieve. I had worked on building this story and its audience for two years, invested countless hours and thousands of dollars, and it was about to die with a barely audible whimper. Worse, it was threatening to take me with it.

I was out of savings, paying creditors with other creditors' money, and working full-time on my own projects in hopes that one might pull through and save me. I now knew that the first of them would not. I had to face the music and get another job if I wanted to keep running, let alone ever get off the ground.

THE STRAITS OF FINANCIAL WOE

THRIFTY TRUCKER

I had been in this situation before. That's what made it so painful. Thankfully, it's also what made it something I could handle, even in my increasingly broken state. I cast off again, ship listing a little too far to port after the most recent beating, hoping against hope the next small island would provide what I needed—at least to repair it.

My friend, Joe, sat me down and walked me through the reasons why I should declare bankruptcy, how it would change everything and help me to get a fresh start.

"My family had to do it a long time ago," he told me. "It was hard on my parents, for sure, but they came out on top in the long run. It changed everything for them and set us up for a better shot than we would have otherwise had."

I saw the wisdom in it but couldn't help feeling ashamed that I couldn't get myself out of trouble. I still believed I could, if only I worked hard enough. If only all that work could be combined with a little good luck.

I was also very, very scared that somehow, that black mark on my record would prevent me from getting back to Paris. I had an emergency fund that I didn't want to touch, air miles dedicated just for my escape, and I was worried that if I raised that black flag and cried for mercy, somehow They would know my plans and They would put a stop to it. Whoever "They" were.

That fear drove me to avoid the question altogether. I put my head down and ignored my friend's incredibly wise advice—I could get myself out of this situation, I told myself. I just needed to keep working.

He put me in touch with a friend of his who ran one of the city's highest-performing dispensaries, and before I knew it, I was selling weed.

LEGALLY.

Here's the kicker: I had never smoked marijuana myself. Yet here I was, working in a store, hawking the stuff to people like I knew what I was talking about.

You might be thinking, "Ha, potheads. Probably not so hard to fool."

In this instance, you would be very wrong. There might have been some light confusion after the boom of variety and availability hit the market, but smokers know their weed and they don't want to waste their money. It wasn't just about smiley-friendly customer service; this job had *ongoing education requirements*.

I hated it. Stepping into an entry-level retail job can be challenging enough as it is in your thirties when you actually care about the product. Organizing an inventory you don't fully understand and working with a bunch of nineteen-year-olds who are suspicious you might really be a cop leads to a lot of demoralizing moments.

Never you mind that the majority of the clientele came in and you immediately wanted to tell them that weed was exactly the last thing they needed to be spending their money on. Half of them looked like they'd just hopped off the most recent freight train passing through town. Most of them seemed about as lost.

The store had to operate completely in cash, as marijuana was still (is still at the time of writing this) federally illegal, which meant that no banks were willing to touch their business. They had an ATM on site briefly until the company caught wind of its exact location and pulled it.

This meant we got paid in cash. It also meant they had to hoard massive amounts of cash for everything including taxes, which were paid in person by the owner, who drove duffel bags full of cash across the state to the capital every couple of weeks for hand delivery.

They even got robbed shortly before I arrived. Weed stores made easy targets in the early days (this may not have changed, for all I know). The main reason they were so tempting, beyond the piles of cash that were likely to be on hand, was that the cops were unlikely to follow up on it.

There's a long history between the police and most of the people involved in the marijuana industry—not a lot of it is friendly. The store I worked at had footage of the robbery sitting on a thumb drive, tacked to the office bulletin board and ready for pickup. Assuming the cops ever took the time to come by and collect the evidence. Which, clearly, they didn't.

Aside from knowing you could get robbed at any moment and the cops gave exactly zero shits about it, the weed store wasn't the worst place to work. It certainly wasn't my favorite, but I was grateful to have it as a side job. At least things were clean and professional, even if the manager ran it like a restaurant and had a habit of sending people home early without warning. With uncertain hours, it was destined to come to an end a month later.

Selling weed also wasn't the only job I picked up. The photo studio I had worked at years before brought me on to do some data-crunching grunt work. I juggled working both jobs as we continued developing Boomerang. Thankfully, I had come to a point in life where I knew better than to marry myself to a job I hated, regardless of my dire circumstances, and I quit selling weed. My short but glorious tenure as a brick-and-mortar drug dealer came to a close, and I swapped the box store for a box truck.

Global Neighborhood Thrift, a charity in Spokane run by a guy I had known since college, was in need of help increasing their donations. They had this big moving truck they could use to pick up donations and a janky system set up on Google Docs to collect requests for donation pickup. But things weren't running smoothly. Their founder, Brent (Studly Mc)Hendricks, knew they

could pull in more donations if the truck was up and running more frequently. But that required a better reservation system and someone dedicated to executing the whole thing.

I thought this was a problem I could solve. It sounded just a little more interesting than selling weed to a rotating cast of train-hopping vagrants. I signed on just before my failed Kickstarter came to its conclusion and got to work collecting people's garbage. I mean donations.

Mostly donations.

PATIENCE IS A LIMITED VIRTUE

Through all of this, I was a pretty brusque character. It's why half the staff at the weed store thought I was a cop (besides being old and balding and constantly saying, "Could you say that again and a little closer to my decorative brooch?"). Being overqualified to work in a job you aren't interested in to begin with while surrounded by people who seem to distrust your very existence isn't a great way to spend any amount of time. Especially when you're only doing so to keep afloat in the midst of pouring your heart into projects that are failing before your eyes. It's among the worst kinds of lifeboats in which you can find yourself.

It also means that the people you're working with are unlikely to be able to empathize with your situation, which leads to some awkward conversations followed by a lot fewer conversations, which feeds into that brusque, untrustworthy persona you seem to be cultivating for yourself. It was better with the photo company; we had a relationship and it was a job with a limited scope, as it was dependent on their spring season. Obviously, the weed store had to go.

But jumping into Global Neighborhood was a treat because even if it wasn't great pay, it still drew on my web-development

abilities and problem-solving skills, and granted me autonomy and some responsibility in an arena that would directly impact the charity. Their mission, in case you haven't gone back to the very beginning of my vlog to see this in action, was to use a thrift store to train recently arrived refugees in American work environments and skills, support them during their language classes and transition period, and then help place them in long-term jobs in the community. It's fantastic work, which added a dash of purpose to rowing in the lifeboat.

That's not to say I returned to my jovial former self—I was still only there to get the job done and then get back to my other work as quickly as possible. But I really liked it. They knew they could grow their business, but the crux of any thrift store's success is the volume of its inbound donations. This was the choke point I was tasked with alleviating.

I set up a new reservation system through their website, organized the times the truck could be active, and then started driving out with a dedicated delivery companion and got to picking up the goods.

We covered the greater Spokane area, driving the truck to clean up after estate sales, yard sales, and drag out random couches people no longer wanted. Things started out slowly— the reservations weren't stacked deep, as they were only being registered by phone at the front counter to start—but once the automated web reservations kicked in, things started picking up.

We canvased neighborhoods while we waited, leaving door hangers on any handle in sight. Notifications started popping on my phone. The calendar started filling up.

It was never that big of a surprise when you showed up to a house and they would take you around back to a shed or open their garage and say, "Have at it." What you found might have been decades' worth of stuff piled up and collecting dust, forgotten

and forlorn. Furniture went in first, with breakables secured at the bottom. Clothes we bagged and tossed on top or shoved anywhere that needed padding.

And we worked fast, often fully loading our truck in fifteen to twenty minutes (depending on the obstacle course set up between the stuff and the truck). Once the truck was full, we'd head back to base, back up to the donations section of the store, and start unloading. It was good exercise. The fact that the donations section was still in a tiny retail office meant we had to be nimble getting through the single glass door. The real joy was in tossing everything onto the pile just beyond it.

We implemented the reservation service late April / early May. June broke all records. July did even better.

That last short paragraph is one of the few moments from this period of my life that I would consider brag-worthy. That and the fact that I somehow survived to write it.

I was still in rough shape, stressing over Boomerang and lamenting the failure of *Into the Nanten's Kickstarter*. In reality, all of that was on the surface—what I was really struggling against was how stuck I felt. I was angry a lot of the time I was alone. Blisteringly so on occasion. I wandered through some really unhealthy and short-lived relationships. My self-respect polled near all-time lows. Desperation began creeping in at the edges—a real sense that I was on a one-way track to heartbroken failure.

I continued to crank away at my other book, *Couriers: OFF GRID*, and I put more and more hope in the success of Boomerang to save me from this personal quagmire. I had fought the shifting currents towards Spokane in the first place, but I had given in, and now I was caught at the center of a massive whirlpool. No matter how hard I pedaled, the curved slope before me never seemed to shift. I needed to get out, and the only way that seemed possible was if Boomerang was a success.

Even if I sold *OFF GRID* to a publisher, I was unlikely to make much, if any, real money. That was the first step in a longer career (that still might not make any money regardless of how long it carried on). If I wanted out, I was going to have to strap together whatever driftwood I could find and attempt to fight my way up and over the swirling water.

But that didn't mean I couldn't send up a signal fire for anyone else out on the nearby seas.

Chapter Nine:

Vlogging to Live

A PHOTO A DAY KEEPS THE DOCTOR POORLY INFORMED

Let's talk about vlogging daily for a minute, because it's the chapter of my life that (most likely) resulted in you picking up a copy of this book in the first place. But in order to understand why the heck a grown-ass man would pick up a camera and make little movies about himself every day for over three years, you've gotta go back and understand that this isn't the first ridiculous thing I've done along these lines.

I had been posting a photo every day for over five years at the point that I started vlogging, closing in on my two thousandth photo of the day. Originally, I launched my daily photos in South Africa as a hackneyed form of journaling but also in hopes of keeping friends and family back home up to date with where I was and what was going on. At the very least, it could serve as proof of life.

What I quickly learned from this experience was that very few people really seemed to care, and fewer gleaned much useful information from my posts.

This was partially due to the limiting nature of a solitary photo to capture the essence of an entire day, partially due to poor captioning, and partially due to a common element in human nature known as apathy.

Leaving aside the average consumer of these photos, whether on Facebook or later Instagram (IG was as yet unavailable on Android), I was most surprised by the people who were actively giving me money to support my work on the ship. There was a shocking number who didn't even know if I was still working for Mercy Ships, let alone what country I was in or what my current job was.

Never mind that I sent out a regular newsletter and updated my blog every week on the same day—I discovered that for the

vast majority of people, "out of sight, out of mind" hits a new extreme when you leave the western world.

Move to Africa and people just assume you're dead.

If not dead, you clearly can't access a phone or the internet, so why bother checking in? It felt reminiscent of the missionaries of old who said goodbye to their families and shipped off with their own casket, despite (hopefully) being decades away from occupying it full-time. There were a lot of people who simply stopped talking to me despite the fact that I still had a functioning mouth and the necessary technology to broadcast its gibberish to the globe.

While challenging, all jokes aside, this is a really important life lesson that I think expatriates get to learn a little more quickly than most: people change and friendships fade. The one constant in the universe, ironically, is change, and that holds especially true for us. There are a few lucky relationships in any life that hold fast across time, distance, and shifting waistlines. Most are for a season. Those seasons accelerate when you leave home, whether for a parent's job, university, or your own job after.

Moving abroad pumps adrenaline into the system. It hurts at first. The hidden blessing is that it teaches you to enjoy what you have while you have it, and that there's nothing wrong with letting go when the time comes.

So, while something like the Photo/Day project couldn't overcome the governing laws of (social?) thermodynamics, it was and continues to be a great exercise in personal discipline. It's a middling success as a personal journal. It's obviously a gaping failure-hole for external communication.

/ cue world's smallest violin

Needless to say, while the project had grown somewhat over time, it wasn't exactly a resounding success in audience-building. I think this was largely because I wasn't using it properly

to tell a story—I never homed in on who that audience should be, either. It wound up being a series of sharp lessons in reality that I only appreciate more over time.

I overcorrected with *Into the Nanten* and focused solely on story, removing myself from it explicitly while pouring my internal struggles into it with painful clarity. That also wasn't working out so well. I needed something in the middle. I didn't need to vanish from the story I wanted to tell; I knew people would like me if they got to know me, call it overconfidence if you must, and I knew that what I was trying to accomplish in life would be interesting to watch if I managed to succeed.

Crashing and burning would be interesting as well, but I sincerely (naively) thought that wasn't likely. I needed something more compelling. And then I discovered Casey Neistat's daily vlog.

CHRONOLOGICAL INACCURACY

That's not entirely true—I didn't discover Casey at this crisis point in my life in Spokane in 2016. I had discovered him while still working as a consultant in Springfield, thanks to my buddy from the ship, Theo. OG vlog viewers might remember "Theodopholus Thursdays"—those were his days (I'm not sure he really noticed this, though—why don't people notice things?!).

Casey, for the three of you who don't know who he is, radically shifted YouTube when he combined vlogging with cinematic shots and montage. They were fast-paced and entertaining, and managed to tell a story every time. I watched him do his thing and immediately thought, *I could do that.* Probably immediately followed by *Why the heck did I never think of this?!*

I wasn't alone. Hundreds of thousands of other people saw what Casey was doing and were inspired. YouTube literally changed as his subscriber count exploded from five hundred

thousand to millions. It was unlike anything that the platform had ever seen. As I'm sure many did, I still consider him my YouTube spiritual mentor.

You might recall that I experimented with vlogging while in Springfield, Spokane, and Taiwan. This was all because of Casey. I had made videos my entire life, but production dropped off steadily as I focused on writing and surviving the crazy travel life that had befallen me. I made skits on the ship, vlogged in Vlog Brothers fashion from Paris, and kept making returns to the format every few months. But I didn't know how to incorporate it into my life in a regular way.

Then Casey's daily vlog hit and I thought, *I have to do this. I need to do this.*

It was hard. I picked up a camera and started filming some of my travels, bits of my daily life, and found it was a *lot* of work. Way more work than I had anticipated, even with a decent sense of filmmaking going in. When I tried vlogging every day for a month back in Paris, the main struggle was coming up with something to say every day. I ran out of ideas after a few weeks.

After a few more years of life experience, this wasn't a major issue anymore. With this new format, the main struggle was pumping out a fully formed mini-movie every day while maintaining a job and the rest of my life. And making sure that each one actually made sense and was at least moderately entertaining. It was killer.

The other hang-up was that I didn't have access to my original YouTube account, on which I had managed to gain some 400 subscribers. I received a mark against my account while living in the Congo, and, unable to access YouTube from the ship or from within the country (not from the ship for bandwidth restrictions, and not from in-country because: dictatorship), I hadn't been able to defend myself and the result was the closure of my entire account. Once I returned from the Congo, YouTube ignored my requests for appeal.

This got fixed completely by chance when on our way to Taiwan, Brian mentioned the situation to our host, who happened to work at YouTube—the infamous Dave who enjoys my videos most when I bleed. He dropped us off at the airport the next morning, then happened to mention it to someone in that department when he got to work. I got a notification on the tarmac at SFO—my account had been restored.

This might sound like no big deal to those of you who have never tried to start a YouTube channel, but they say the first one thousand subscribers are the hardest to get. This is true, but only after the first hundred. I now had four hundred, even if most of them had forgotten I existed by this point.

The other thing about Casey's vlog that resonated with me was the strategy behind it—he was building an audience for a tech company he was preparing to launch. Even as he went to investors at the time, he was pitching it as a strength. A unique point that made them more likely to succeed.

I had a tech company I wanted to get out to the world too. In the long term, I wanted to better share my fiction projects like *Into the Nanten*.

Considering how hard ITN had been to produce, and expensive, I needed something I was passionate about that I could accomplish entirely on my own. Something more shareable than journal entries from an exiled warrior. Video, being one of my oldest passions and simultaneously the king of content, seemed like a no-brainer iteration to me.

Still, I wasn't deluded. I knew that my odds were long and that there was no controlling the success of what I was about to set out to do. Knowing that turning YouTube into a profession was likely a pipe dream, and something that would happen a long ways down the road if at all, I sat down and wrote out some professional goals around the vlog.

I wanted to tell a story with every video, make one and upload it every day, and do so for at least one year. I also wrote out some personal goals, which included the following (I literally copied and pasted this out of the original document):

- Overcome insecurity in filming myself in public - especially talking to the camera;
- Overcome insecurity in being goofy - voices - singing - being myself;
- Learn to voice opinions without letting fear prevent or nerf my thoughts (use a filter still, please);
- Learn to backflip from standing;
- Get good at longboarding;
- Master the schedule - be disciplined in your time;
- Master drone flying;
- Overcome self-doubt in your value as a creator and human being;
- Overcome insecurities surrounding status and appearance - again, learn your value;
- Master your finances - overcome the insecurities that come with financial stress and be responsible with what you have.

I did put some effort into the backflip lessons early on, but I need to get back to that someday soon. More importantly at the time, I knew that if I did things correctly, I'd be making a much richer journal of my life to look back on. I could communicate who I was and where I wanted to go much more clearly and pull people along for the ride.

What I didn't realize was just how scared I still was to do any of this.

PIRATES MUTINEERS

EXTERNAL
NAY-SAYERS
ILLEGITIMIZERS
MOOCHERS
HATERS
OBSEQUIENTS
USERS

INTERNAL
DOUBT
SELF-SABOTAGE
FEAR
PRIDE
FATIGUE
ENTITLEMENT

A GLIMMER IN THE GLOOM

I started vlogging on June 6th, 2016, the day I posted my two thousandth photo of the day. I lined things up so that when I uploaded the video the following day, Vlog a Day 1 hit alongside Photo/Day 2,001. It made keeping the count easier, especially since I have to recalibrate my Photo/Day count every year as it inevitably wanders off the mark (again, no one notices, but I'm fine with the lack of scrutiny on certain occasions).

My sister, Kaarin, and her husband, Kevin, helped me film all of the intro characters on that first day, which coincidentally made for quite the first vlog. Kevin, also a video professional, didn't believe we could get it all done in a day. I'll remind him of that until the day he dies (hi, Kevin).

The intro characters, for those of you who have wondered, were originally going to be a set of photos for ridiculous head shots to hand out at conventions. I was still attending conventions at this point, hand-selling both seasons of *Into the Nanten* in hopes of finding a larger audience for that future relaunch (and, of course, I'd reserved my space at a lot of the conventions in hopes that the third season would be launching in the fall). I grew my beard out for months with the plan to carve it into different shapes, don different costumes, and take a bunch of photos in the guise of various famous authors from history.

It simply never came together. But as the idea of the vlog grew in my mind, so too did the thought that I could use my beard for an even greater cause. And so, the intro characters were birthed into existence through some haphazard shaving on the go.

I worked at a thrift store, so costuming was cheap if a little creative. My sister and brother-in-law helped keep me on track when spouting out all of the numbers, as well as making the actual filming much easier and less stressful than doing it on my own (something I would experience the following year). They were amazing. The whole thing came together over the span of eight hours. And then I sat down to edit.

Vlogging for me didn't feel so much like work in those early days as like a joyful release. I was stuck in a city I didn't think even wanted to try and understand me, struggling to realize a dream I had for my future that no one else saw. Even as I picked up some freelance writing gigs and helped one of my best friends on shoots for his growing production company, I didn't have any real creative outlet that had hopes of being gratified.

Very few people bought art from my display in Coeur. Like, way too few. I did find a new and amazing fan through the display and the books we slowly sold from the mantel—Keleren, you were

a saving grace—but overall, my efforts were met with disinterest or straight-up eye-rolls.

Into the Nanten had come to a full halt, meaning that I was no longer writing regularly or managing that team. I was increasingly depressed, struggling to care or feel more than angry despair.

This is why I say that vlogging saved me—because in many ways, it did. I suddenly had a creative outlet that was fresh every day. The challenges were new, the story different, and the results finished before I went to bed. Even though very few people watched back then (thanks, Jeff, Slush, and Dad), the gratification was practically instant in the limited response I received. I really, really enjoyed it.

More than that, I saw that I had the potential to do it well.

Daily vlogging, especially with any attempt at production value, is a herculean effort. On an average day, I woke up around 7 AM, filmed, worked, filmed while working, ate, filmed that too, worked job number two or three, did Boomerang stuff, edited, and then went to bed around 2 AM. Every day. I averaged five to six hours of sleep for a long time. It wasn't healthy, but it was reinvigorating.

There was a fresh purpose to even the smallest elements of any given day. Doing laundry? How could I best capture that and make it interesting. . . Loading the truck with donations? How could I angle a fun time-lapse, or make it look like I was tossing bags onto the pile at superhuman speed. . .

My energy went up for other projects. I kept toiling away at *OFF GRID*, applying the first round of notes from a friend at the publisher in hopes that it would make a stronger proposal to the entire team. I dove even harder into Boomerang. The stress was mounting, and I wasn't making it easier on myself by adding a vlog to the mix, but I needed it.

Even if few outside my family really got it, or at least put up with it, there were people outside Spokane who did. People out

on the internet, in Seattle or LA or all the way over in Eindhoven, the Netherlands. Suddenly, I had a link to a world that, even if they didn't fully understand me, got excited and supported me anyway.

It made the sideways glances and dismissals tolerable in person. I was making something for me—something I would enjoy editing that night and have fun getting feedback on in the morning. My dad and my buddy Slush were quick to tell me that things got boring if I stretched beyond six to seven minutes (hard to believe that used to be my hard cap). Jeff pushed me to show more pizza. Suddenly, there was a dialog around my work, small as it was, and I could see steady improvements in it.

More importantly, there were people out there who were willing to show up and be a part of it every day, even as I figured out what I was doing.

I regained a sense of optimism for my future I had steadily lost. I gained a handful of subscribers up front. Even as I entered a few-month period where I didn't gain a single additional subscriber (yikes, I know), I was happy to be making videos. It was basically another unpaid part-time job, but for once, there was a ray of sunshine in the mix.

AN ISLAND PLATFORM

Even though the vlog gave me something to hold on to, and a way of communicating over the event horizon of my little whirlpool of death—as with any whirlpool of death—I still needed out of the whirlpool of death.

My lifeline came from the most unexpected of places, a very small island deep in the Caribbean.

St. Vincent and the Grenadines, despite sounding like a barbershop quartet comprised of freewheeling monks, is a chain of islands not far from the coast of Venezuela. The largest of

these, St. Vincent, is home to the capital, Kingstown. The smallest inhabited island, Mayreau, is located some hours away by ferry, and it was to this small island I was called.

Literally called.

I was on the dock at Global Neighborhood unloading someone's owl-lamp collection from the truck when my phone started ringing. It was my old boss, Bryce, who you may remember from my escapades into Switzerland while working for Mercy Ships Global. That goal of his to build a resort on an island in the Caribbean had made great strides. The story itself was nuts, how he'd been on his honeymoon decades prior and said offhand that he would one day own part of the island they were passing for the very purpose of supporting struggling volunteers.

Later, it turned out that the woman who owned a huge chunk of that very island was indeed looking to sell. And then at the last minute, rather than follow through with the agreed-upon price of some $2+ million, she opted to give it to him for free.

This is the kind of stuff that follows Bryce around whistling, the Pied Piper of generous patrons.

Fast forward to 2016: the staff house was finished and in need of babysitting. He didn't have anyone to stay in the house for a six-week stint later in the summer, and he wanted someone to do just that and supervise the delivery of his regular shipping container. I didn't know how on earth I could make that work. I was working part-time for a charity, so I wasn't exactly rolling deep, but I knew I needed to return to a seaward trajectory. And soon. Perhaps this real island was my chance to escape the whirlpool, the boost I needed to carry me to the metaphorical island where we would launch Boomerang and, possibly, the rest of my voyage.

I'm not sure if *escape velocity* describes what boats need in these situations, but it was certainly what I was looking for. And why not attach rockets to the side of a ship? I mean, there are

reasons, but things were looking desperate and this seemed like the perfect first-stage booster to me. I said yes, I'd do it, and began prepping to head south.

So, It Turns Out Mosquitoes Are Real

August 12, 2016, literally four days before I flew to the island, I got my official rejection from the publisher for *OFF GRID*. Out on the open ocean, with no land in sight and no hope of resupply, I had three destinations I hoped might work out. Three islands that, if they only held one of the treasures marked on my map, could keep me from giving up and being forced back.

Now two of them had failed to materialize. I was devastated but wouldn't let myself feel it. Not yet. Instead, I put all or nothing on the third.

I lined up what ducks were necessary, bought tickets with my deep air-miles reserve, and put Spokane in the rearview mirror with no intentions of ever coming back for more than a visit.

For one, Mayreau sounded like an amazing backdrop for my vlog, a change of scenery that might interest more people than Spokane. For two, it was not Spokane. And that's not *entirely* intended as a jab at Spokane.

There was still a sense of safety in Spokane, of second options and bail-out plans. Maybe what I needed was to distance myself from those and really focus on Boomerang as my only option. I had been working on another book, *Agnar's Box*, and while I was in love with the idea, maybe writing needed to take a back seat for now.

Despite the uncertainty in my future, there was a sense of release when I boarded that first flight for the Caribbean. It was a familiar adventure, stepping into a new culture in a country I'd never visited, and I desperately needed an adventure like that. I

had muscles wasting away that needed flexing. It felt like progress. I was exiting the whirlpool.

I made some of the best videos of my vlog on that trip—with broken-down cars and near-misses on ferries. Beyond the excitement for something new and my restored pride in being able to tackle it, I felt like I was coming back to life in some small way. The burden of the giant risks I was taking were ever-present. The weight of my most recent failure pulled so much harder on me than I ever let on when talking to the camera, along with the knowledge that I was only one more failure away from complete collapse.

Or deflation. Wherever I had previously been in life, between both coasts and the Midwest of the US, the southern tip of Africa or its sub-Saharan jungles, I had never had any problems with mosquitoes. If they bit me, I didn't know it. But the mosquitoes in the Caribbean had fire on their tongues. I felt every bite, for a solid thirty minutes, and it was not the adventure I was looking for. Bryce had an electrified racket through which I channeled my rage and avenged every bite with a thousand tiny mosquito deaths!

Sorry, flashbacks there for a second.

The island was tiny, visited by ferries from the bigger islands only every few days, and thus quite isolated. What was even more isolating was the house rule that I couldn't bring anyone inside—hard to make friends when you can't invite them over. There was a house dog, however, Indy, who became my fast companion and escorted me everywhere I went so long as it didn't involve crossing paths with the main pack of dogs in the middle of town. If that was on the table, she'd opt to meet me back at home.

I settled in for a six-week retreat and got ready to launch the Kickstarter for Boomerang.

THE FIRST GUSTS OF CHANGE

I made a critical error in how I presented this period of my life in the vlog: I didn't share how important any of these projects were to me. When *Into the Nanten* came to a screeching halt, I died a little on the inside. On the vlog, I talked about it like it was no big deal. We'd get back to it eventually—I said—but I kept looking forward to the future.

When *OFF GRID* received its final blow from the publisher, I was deeply disappointed. I didn't take it as a personal rejection, but it threw up a massive roadblock on my hopeful path forward. I remember hiking up the slope of the island, thinking about how I wished I could share just how much it hurt, and deciding to put on a strong face instead. I didn't want people to see a failure when they saw me, I wanted them to revel in the glories of my success.

To keep the metaphor alive: I had come to impassable reefs twice in a matter of months, I was running desperately low on supplies, and I was refusing to tell what little crew I had just how bad things really were.

I thought if I just brushed it off, moved forward, and succeeded on the next thing, that would be good enough. No one wants to hear a sob story, I figured; they just want to see you soar. I didn't want to show just how precarious my position was. I didn't want my failures to define me.

While this is perfectly normal; it makes for poor storytelling. My few viewers didn't really know how important these things were to me because I was hiding it from them, so, naturally, it didn't seem to be a big deal to them when things didn't go well.

I continued to hide as we prepared to launch Boomerang.

The first couple of weeks passed slowly in my relative isolation on the island. I spent my time building the website, Kickstarter campaign, and trying to coordinate a shoestring-budget

PR push. There were also many quick mosquito-killing sprees that got me up and out of my chair for some necessary exercise. I ran with Indy on the beach, made my daily vlog, and tried to enjoy myself as much as circumstances would allow.

Then something interesting happened: I could sense a change in the winds.

While I had struggled to fight the pull of the whirlpool of my circumstances, spiritually, internally, I had been sitting on still waters. Not the kind of still waters you relax beside, but *still*, windless conditions out at sea, where all I've got to work with for propulsion are sails, and all sails can use for fuel is wind. I may have been putting up a fight, externally refusing to give up and continuing to knuckle down day after day. But internally, I lost all momentum. I had been dead in the water for months.

The desire to get back to Paris, my hopes for a publishing career, even the dream that my videos on YouTube might one day go somewhere—all of that had stagnated. And yet, after a few weeks on the lam, away from the weight of whatever it was that smothered me while consulting or strangled me in Spokane, I felt the slightest breeze pick up across the surface of my soul.

There was a sudden pull, however slight. A desire to return to Paris, which stood out to me as a glimmer of burgeoning health. I hadn't felt that pull to Paris in months, perhaps a couple of years. I didn't know where it was coming from, but I took it as a sign. There was a chance I might yet recover, and the odds were clearly better back in the City of Lights.

ABANDON SHIP

Three weeks of mosquito-bitten isolation is enough to make anyone question their life choices. Even the net over my bed suffered a number of security breaches—it must be a mosquito's

dream to have an entire human trapped, unconscious, and all to itself for eight hours. The house itself was wonderfully built, with an add-on for the local maintenance guy and a massive deck with a view of the mountainous island across the way. Hammocks galore. They just hadn't made it possible to keep the little bloodsuckers out.

Between welted mosquito-slaying rage sessions, I got as much work done as possible in the heat. The Kickstarter campaign and our product website had really come together. The renderings of our final version of the bracelet looked slick—the 3-D printed versions turning out wonderfully, if not quite finished enough.

When we dove into the project, we had a few decisions to make surrounding our strategy. Each team member put in $5,000, totaling $25,000 between the five of us, from which we withdrew whatever money we needed for the project. This was enough money to get our prototypes built, some basic design work and photography done, our trip to Taiwan to set up manufacturing, etc. But in order to truly market the product, or get finished versions we could photograph and send out for trials, would have cost tens of thousands more.

We opted not to look for investment, nor to bring a completely realized product to market, but to lean into the tried-and-true Kickstarter ethos of crowdfunding a nearly complete idea. We had functioning prototypes and mock-ups for everything we wanted to achieve; we just needed a little help getting across the finish line. It was one path we could choose among a few, and it came with its own set of pros and cons.

We were lean, the risk to us personally was low, and we hadn't sold any part of our company to outside influence. The challenge was that we had no budget for marketing, the product looked a little rough, and we had to ask for the full amount we actually needed to move to production. As Kickstarter is an all-or-

nothing platform, if we didn't make that full amount, we'd be dead in the water—where if we had an investor come in and pay half of that amount up front or more, we could have asked for much less from the public and thus increased the chances of continuing on.

Originally, we wanted to launch in May, which was why I had felt comfortable moving in with my parents and focusing so heavily on it instead of getting another EMR gig. That hopeful deadline got pushed to June, then July.

By the time I got the itch to fly back to Paris from Mosquito Island, it was late August. Our final launch date was set for September 14th. The container delivery I was supposed to supervise had also been delayed, leaving me with no real responsibilities on the island. Bryce kindly said I could depart. I was ready to go in every sense.

YOU DIDN'T THINK THERE WOULD BE POKÉMON IN THIS BOOK, DID YOU?

This provided the ultimate opportunity for a surprise visit to my friends in Paris. But how does one go about leaving an island in a secretive fashion when one posts one's life on the internet every day for all to see?

The answer: Pokémon.

Pokémon GO was still all the rage and I had made mention of it occasionally in my vlog as a family activity. Viewers had asked if there were any good Pokémon on the island (there weren't) and what kind of exotic variety might be at my disposal (literally no Pokémon), and I had been intending to make a joke video about this very subject for a while. It served as the ultimate smoke screen for my departure.

If you haven't seen the video in question, it went a little like this: With everything packed, the house locked down tight,

and Indy snuggled goodbye, I begin hunting for Pokémon across the island. Not finding any near the house, on the beach below, nor the heights above, I suddenly, inexplicably, decide to hop the local school ferry and try the next island over. The next island has no Pokémon either, shockingly, and so I buy a plane ticket on the spot and make for an even BIGGER island.

You can see where this is going, but on the vlog—for the few people watching at the time—it seemed genuinely bonkers that I would suddenly up and start island-hopping in search of Pokémon. What they couldn't see (with the exception of one shot that I left in for posterity) was that my camera was sitting on top of my full luggage for every shot. I was leaving the island, but I told no one save for Bryce and my sister. I wanted the rest to be a surprise.

This was the tension I had always hoped to build with the *Into the Nanten* entries. Now I could aim to create a joyfully confused applause with my own life. I ended that day's vlog with a failed hunt for Pokémon in Barbados and woke up the next day demanding a flight somewhere new.

Chapter Ten:
Rock Bottom

AH, PARIS

If you're thinking this is the part where I get to Paris and we spend the rest of the book celebrating, you could be forgiven for all the buildup. I did, technically, make it to Paris. But this was only temporary—on a standard tourist visa—with no concrete plans of staying. There was a tech company to continue building, a Bluetooth bracelet to get into production, and marketing efforts to make in order to get well and truly on the map.

Either way, it was refreshing to land in Paris in the second week of September. Paris in the fall is an easy favorite, as it seamlessly combines two of my favorite institutions. I saw friends, took long strolls, and even got taken to Crazy Horse (an infamously intense cabaret) on a first date by a French woman I met on the Métro. There was so much happening—the city felt alive and I channeled that energy as best I could. Returning to Paris for the first time in three years put things into fresh perspective.

It felt like coming home.

As I'm sure happens for a thousand different people every day, strolling the streets reminded me how much I wanted to make Paris my base. The crisp air and colorful leaves falling against an Haussmannian backdrop revitalized a broader vision for my future after years of narrowing my focus to survive. It reminded me of something I had nearly forgotten: I had to get back here.

But first, we had to get Boomerang off the ground. My landlady kindly let me operate out of her dining room so that I wasn't trapped using Starbucks Wi-Fi again. I continued plugging away on Boomerang over twelve-hour days to get ready, still managing to get out and make vlogs as I went. If we managed to get Boomerang off the ground, it might not lead back to Paris anytime soon, but at least I would have a clear path.

I could go on salary with the company relatively quickly, build the product for the next five to ten years, and work my way to independence. I could be free. All we had to do was pull off this first round of funding via Kickstarter and we would be on our way. We needed just over $50,000—it would be enough to keep everything afloat a little while longer. Including me.

We pulled the trigger on September 14th, 2016.

By September 15th, I knew we were faceplanting.

We got almost all the support we would get within the first twenty-four hours, and, to me, the inevitable was immediately apparent. I sat in my landlady's apartment, emailing news outlets and pumping out what social plugs I could manage. We were met with stony silence on all fronts.

I had made it to the third island, coasting in on the last rickety breath of my ship before it collapsed in the shallows. Stumbling to shore with my shovel, I found the spot marked on my map. The X was the biggest on any of the maps I'd yet brought with me. The dig was difficult, the sand giving way to rock far too quickly. And suddenly, with desperate clarity, I realized that rock was all I would uncover. I let the map fall from my hand and flutter off in a breeze, far too aware of how badly my ship needed repairs. How little food and water remained in my stores.

How all hopes of resupply were now lost, let alone treasure. I had spent it all and I had nothing left to show for it.

AH, DAMNIT

I sat staring at my computer, willing the numbers to rise on our campaign. Wishing they'd go higher so I could stop doing random side jobs and struggling to pay my debts. Desperate to keep from being cast back to the Shores of the Known and shipwrecked.

My powers of persuasion proved insufficient. Our campaign barely budged for the next month until we finally decided to pull the plug and regroup.

We would never fully regroup.

Leaving Paris was painful. I had already purchased space with my old buddy Mike at a convention in Minneapolis to sell our books, so there was something to look forward to as I packed up, but I didn't know if or when I would ever make it back. It had taken me years just to visit.

My friend Chinwe pushed me to make an effort while we drove across the city near the end of my trip. "If you can get back to Paris, I'll get you a job teaching English at my school."

"But will they sponsor me?" I asked. "I can't just show up and start working on a tourist visa."

"No," she said. "But if you get legal, you'll have work."

This was also the ride on which she told me, offhandedly, "You look much more handsome on camera than in person." So, it was a winner of a trip all around.

The age-old catch-22. You can't move to France and work without a working visa, but you can't get a working visa without already having a job to sponsor you. . .and you'll pretty much never get a job without being there to look for one in the first place (cue throwing your hands in the air and walking into the forest).

The one card I had up my sleeve was my old apartment—I had an address in Paris already, which made jumping through some hoops easier. It also significantly reduced the cost of making the move—no security deposit, no rent. But it didn't help get me a job or a visa. And then I thought, *Why not go for that Holy Grail of a visa I've heard about?*

When I'd first poked around trying to stay in France before, I stumbled across this visa called "Compétences et talents," which was a visa for artists and entrepreneurs to stay and work on their projects in France.

There was no way I would qualify. I had no big publisher behind me, and my entire career was based on my own self-promotion. But I also had nothing to lose if they said no.

Ah, Down We Go

Minneapolis is a city covered in sky bridges and drunken zombies. That's been a lot of my experience, at least, and I have zero complaints about it. I'll revisit over Halloween any year— if only NerdCon: Stories, the convention that brought me back, hadn't been cancelled after that year.

Making a stopover in Chicago immediately after was also a cathartic last hurrah as I circled the drain. I dropped into the Windy City to see friends and apply for my shot-in-the-dark visa at the consulate. Or so I thought—I wasn't allowed to because it wasn't *my* consulate. I lived in the wrong region, which meant it was going to require a totally separate trip to San Francisco.

My momentum stalled out. I had been using my pile of air miles to travel, to regain some sense of sanity, but I only had enough left for one trip back to Paris. I couldn't burn them on the requisite stop in San Francisco.

That first blow to my hopes was followed quickly by the realization that I had to get another job if I was going to stay afloat for a few more months. Maybe even longer, if I couldn't figure out how to escape. My friends in Chicago offered to put me up for a while if I found work in EMR, jobs which were available, if sparse. But they wouldn't be temporary—and what I needed had to be temporary or I risked being completely waylaid. After a brief moment in Paris, a return to a career in EMR sounded like the equivalent of setting my damaged ship ablaze just to have a nice bonfire for the evening.

It was in the midst of this research spree in Chicago that I got a perfectly timed message from a friend whose cousin needed help with his growing staging company back in Spokane. With nowhere else to turn, mounting bills, and all of my big projects dumped in the failure bin, I made the call and got another job moving furniture into trucks.

AH, MY BACK

Moving furniture is good work; don't get me wrong. Doing so for a staging company is surprisingly satisfying. The idea behind staging is simple: most homes on the market are empty, but homes that feel well-furnished and lived-in sell better. It's easier to imagine what you would do with a room if you can see how someone else put it together (even if it's just to spark the thought *I would never do it like that*). Empty rooms feel cold and uninviting, and uninviting houses aren't the kind most people are looking to buy.

So, we staged homes that were up for sale, renting them the furniture for as long as it took, and their odds of selling went up significantly. The process was essentially this: fill up a trailer with a predetermined furniture set, drive it to the house, set it up as quickly as possible, and sprint back to the warehouse to do it all over again. That or head to a house that had recently sold and pack up its furniture to be used in another one nearby.

I saw the inside of a lot more houses. Thankfully, this time, most of them were clean, and none of our pickups involved piles of garbage bags masquerading as merchandise while filled with moldy memorabilia.

The couple that owned the company were industrious and hardworking. They were also a lot younger than me.

Coming off a string of what felt like career-ending failures heightened my awareness to contrasts like this. And it wasn't just them—a big challenge was not comparing myself to anyone around me. Even if I didn't want the lives of the people surrounding me, I still couldn't have achieved them if I wanted. I would have gone insane in the attempt. My apparent inability to succeed at any of my own projects, at finding my route across the Unknown, seemed inescapable.

I was running out of energy. Worse, I was losing the last shreds of hope I'd held.

Where I'd spent a lot of time screaming at Springfield as I drove around, my loathing turned more pointedly inward in Spokane. That's not to let Spokane entirely off the hook, but it is significantly better than being stuck in Springfield, Illinois. Now that I think about it, I can see why Honest Abe went through everything he did just to leave. But I digress.

Spokane still fostered an environment that bent my frustrations back in on me. The darker thoughts that had brewed below the surface for some time began bubbling out in private moments. "If I'm really stuck on this ride, if this is all that life has to offer, I'd rather get off."

Every day spent assembling, packing, and staging furniture brought a deeper sense of futility. There was a never-ending pile of repetitive work to do and it didn't matter; I wasn't making enough money to make any difference in my situation regardless of how many couches I assembled. It didn't help that I was helping people buy and sell houses—the ultimate symbol of unattainable promises within the American dream. At least for me and many like me.

I wasn't suicidal—I never contemplated killing myself—but that's not to say I didn't wish I were dead on occasion. I certainly came to understand those who struggle with suicidal thoughts more than I ever had before. If I had hit the cap on all life had to offer me, if I was going to be prevented from pursuing my passions at every front for the rest of time, then I preferred to just cut my losses.

On every level, I was facilitating the dreams of others, unable to make headway on my own.

The statistics showed I wasn't alone. They say Gen X is the first generation of Americans whose prospects are worse than their parents—and I belong to a generation that has it even worse—but despite the generational solidarity, I felt very alone. Having worked in a marketing company for a payday loan company and in a weed

dispensary, I'd witnessed just how tight and inescapable this cycle could become, but I never considered that I could ever be at risk myself.

Education and hard work—these were the keys to the American dream as I understood it. I had an education, but in the new landscape, it was the wrong specialty for desirable jobs and left me overqualified for what was left. So, I knuckled down and leaned into the Puritanical promises of a dedicated work ethic. But the harder I worked, the further my dreams seemed from me.

The promises of my youth had come to nothing.

Thankfully, through all of this, I had a roof over my head and meals provided by my parents. They couldn't afford to do much else, but they lent me a car so I could get to work and they gave me a bed so I had a place to sleep. In the midst of what felt like a cascade of failures and endless false starts, it was easy to lose sight of just how lucky I was to have them. I can only imagine how much more devastatingly overwhelming the struggle would have been without them.

And then my dad pulled out the big guns and went above and beyond what would have been possible for many in my situation: he used his own miles with Alaska Airlines and got me a round-trip ticket to San Francisco to visit the consulate and apply for my Holy Grail visa. He tossed me one final lifeline, and with it I was able to pull myself onto a rickety ship that would either make it out to sea or sink in the attempt.

I was more than willing to take that risk.

SFO to CDG

This story has been told on occasion, but I'm not sure if all at once or in one place. I'll start by saying I'm eternally grateful to my dad for giving me the push I needed to follow through on the

visa process. He saw the final barrier of getting there for what it was: just the final barrier. He's amazing, my dad—you should meet him; you'd like him.

I flew to San Francisco for my appointment and stayed with Dave, the guy who reinstated my YouTube account and gets referenced in my vlog anytime I bleed. And let's be honest, he's earned the occasional bloody nod. Staying with him over New Year's was a great distraction from the madness that was about to consume my life.

HOW TO APPLY FOR A FRENCH VISA AND NOT GO INSANE

Applying for a visa used to be a process that happened within consulates. It's changed in the last few years, so this won't necessarily reflect current reality, but I think most of the concepts remain the same. Those working in consulates, in my experience, are about ten times nicer than the ones you run into at the prefecture, but better to be mentally prepared.

First of all: Attitude

You are at the mercy of the bureaucrat before you and you should act like you know it. Smile; be kind but deferential. Make sure you have everything listed as necessary in whatever documentation they've given you. In the embassy/consulate scenario, this should suffice. At the prefecture, it won't. They'll always have something else "you should have known" to bring. This is bullshit. You can't say it's bullshit. You just smile and ask for further clarification on whatever you need to bring with you next time and swallow your pride.

As for the consulate, things went very smoothly. They weren't interested in copies of my books, or any additional proof I

was remotely recognized in my field. They just wanted to check all the appropriate boxes and move on to the next person.

What threw a wrench in the gears was when they looked in their process book and couldn't find the visa for which I was applying.

Second thing: Perseverance

"What?" I said in French, face twitching to betray just how not well I was taking the news.

"It's not here," he repeated, also in French, flipping through the three-ring binder. "What was it called again?"

"Compétences et talents," I croaked, cleared my throat, and repeated with what might have sounded like confidence. This was my true competence. . .or talent. . .

The consulate worker flipped back through the pages. "I still don't see it."

"It's on your website," I said a little too quickly. "That's where I found it."

"OK." He seemed more perplexed than perturbed. "I'll look."

I started sweating under my jacket. It gets cold in San Francisco—they don't tell you that when you live in Washington State—you assume every part of California is blazing hot. It's not, at least not yet. You have to learn it for yourself on your first trip and then never forget again. "It's not listed on the main page for some reason, but if you search for it, you'll find it."

"I still don't see it," he said as he scanned the list.

"Search for it on Google," I repeated. "You'll find it." *Please find it.*

"OK," he shrugged. I remember thinking I'd struck the rarest square in French Bureaucrat Bingo.

"Compétences et talents, San Francisco," I said for probably

the tenth time as I tried to guide him towards the page that would make or break me.

"Ah," he said in that curt-yet-pleasant way that marks French satisfaction. "Here it is. Let me. . ." He literally highlighted the entire webpage, copied it, pasted it into a Word document, and printed it out. "There we go. Let's begin."

He processed my application off a printout of a webpage he only found because I walked him to it. I should have bought a lotto ticket. The only other hiccup was not having a suitable self-addressed, prepaid, trackable envelope for them to return my passport to me—that's right; they keep your passport—but that was easy enough to fix. It doesn't mean I wasn't breathless with stress as I sprinted to the post office and screamed, "SOMEONE GIVE ME AN ENVELOPE." But it worked out.

The third thing: Accepting mystery

"Will they accept me or won't they?" is only the first of a long series of unanswerable questions on which you'll have the delight of stewing. There's no way of knowing. In my case, after three weeks, I got so nervous I finally wrote them an email to ask, only to discover they had sent an email I never received.

The visa for which I had applied no longer existed. You might imagine this doesn't engender an initial boost of positive emotions.

In fact, this causes immediate spikes of anxiety. It's nearing the end of January. You're back to the painfully endless downward spiral in a town you've tried multiple times to leave behind. You've been waiting for weeks to find out if this cycle will end—lacing your job and social commitments with extra doses of uncertainty. These are not words you want to hear.

But lose not all hope! At least not yet—because they're developing a new visa at the embassy, and the consulate workers think you stand a chance at getting it. They can't really tell you anything about it, and you suspect you're a guinea pig for their own perverse paper-pushing curiosities, but you jump at the opportunity to have your case sent on to the embassy. Experiment of convenience or no, this is the single kindest moment in French bureaucratic history.

The embassy sends you an austere email a week later asking only for "More financial documents." You put together the most complimentary packet of financial information a couch-lugging, self-published, going-nowhere-on-YouTube-YouTuber can manage. It contains no lies, but it certainly contains little context.

They buy it.

The email comes through, asking, "When do you want to arrive in France?"

It's February 17th. Your status with the airline runs out on March 1st—this is important because you're allowed four oversized bags on an overseas flight with this level of status, and you're moving.

"February 28th" is the only possible response. You hit Send, you use the last of your air miles to book a one-way ticket, and you pray they get your passport back to you in time.

There's a level of disbelief and uncertainty that follows a moment like this. *Is it real?* I don't even know the name of the visa, nor how long it's for… *Can I work?* I was sitting at the window in Vessel, a coffee shop in Spokane that I'm not 100% sure is still in business. Traffic on Monroe Street continued streaming past, gray clouds sliding overhead. I considered drafting an email with my various questions. I opted against it for fear they would finally spot me for the impostor I was.

Either way—I couldn't help the steady rush of joy that sprung up through my gut.

I almost shouted and danced my way across the coffee shop, spinning strangers in place, spilling drinks and scattering coffee merch across the floor. Instead, I packed up silently, slung my bag over my shoulder, and stepped out into the crisp winter air, grinning like an idiot. I was headed back to Paris.

CHAPTER ELEVEN:

CREATING AND PATREON

HUSKY CASES FOR HUSKY TRAVELERS

I was elated. Excited. Ecstatic. I was escaping.

I also needed more luggage. Luggage is expensive. You know what isn't? Plastic cases built to store tools. In a bid to see how far I could push my "oversized/overweight" luggage allowance, I went out and bought a huge hard-plastic Husky tub on wheels and filled it to the maximum allowed. The ticket agent didn't even blink.

I traveled with five bags, 210 pounds in total, and never enjoyed the struggle more. I grinned through security. I chuckled as I transferred. I skipped my way to customs.

There was an awkward moment where the immigration officer didn't recognize my visa; it was so new, the embassy didn't even have any documentation to send me, but they shrugged, took some notes, and stamped me through. I WAS IN.

I got to my tiny apartment, shoved my oversized luggage in storage, and was good and truly free.

What was evident in my vlog were a lot of the smaller challenges and some of the big ones. One very real challenge was my computer's rapidly deteriorating health. The battery had swollen in the heat of the Caribbean, leaving me with a grand total of fifteen minutes of life untethered from the nearest outlet. Not a big deal as long as I left it plugged in, but it made editing on the go a massive challenge. What made editing as a whole even more difficult was when the keyboard had a stroke.

I took my laptop into the local repair shop to see if there was anything that could be done for my power issues. His response was to unplug the battery—that way, there wouldn't be any problem so long as I kept it plugged into the wall. What he also unplugged, before sealing the computer back up, was half of the keyboard. I had to edit an entire video with half of my keyboard

not working—through a combination of creative mouse skills and the use of the on-screen accessibility keyboard. I was at that repair shop again first thing in the morning.

While that and bigger struggles, like getting through the immigration process, made it immediately into my vlog, my work and money situations did not. I was still terrified to tell anyone just how precarious my position was. But much like the first time I'd moved to Paris, I had a job lined up and I just needed to survive long enough to get paid.

And much like the first time I'd moved to Paris, nothing went the way it was supposed to from the get-go.

ENGLISH MAKES A BETTER WINDOW THAN A DOOR

As you may recall, my friend Chinwe didn't just let me know how disappointing my appearance was in reality. She had also promised to hook me up with a job teaching English as soon as I made it (legally) to France. Many Americans think that being a native English speaker, perhaps with a degree or two in the right direction, will make it easy to get a job teaching English in a country like France that obviously needs a little help.

This is unfortunate folly. There are plenty of English speakers in the UK and Ireland who are happy to jump over to Europe and already legally able to do so (although this is getting shaken up for obvious reasons). No one is falling over themselves to hire any Americans. I was lucky to have this opportunity.

It was March; I had just a little money left over on which to survive (and a little wiggle room left across a few credit cards). Chinwe's boss wouldn't even meet with me until I had a formalized business structure in place.

I took it in stride. I had no idea what I was doing or if I was even technically allowed to open a business in France because,

as you may recall, THEY DIDN'T TELL ME. Was I allowed to work at all? No one had told me what my visa was good for—how long it would last—or what its limitations were. I was completely in the dark. Opening a business seemed like the perfect way to get found out. Discovered. Called out for the fraud and lawbreaker I might have been.

And yet, I had no choice.

This process reintroduced me to one of the great ongoing struggles with living in France: where to find reliable information. I went into my local mayor's office, who gave me a piece of paper with a phone number, which led me to a website to make an appointment to open the equivalent of a sole proprietorship. But I couldn't figure out for the life of me how to find the phone number on the website itself. I had to call two more offices before someone told me that I had to click on the little map of France in the corner on the website in order to get to the phone numbers.

Read all the sarcasm in the world into the following four words: *well, that makes sense.*

Make an appointment. Keep the appointment. Have no answers for the lady helping you set things up because you really have no idea what you're doing. Thankfully, she seems to believe you have every right to be there. Walk out with a fairly unofficial piece of paper that says you've started a business and an assurance that the official one isn't far behind.

Profit.

I got in for my interview at the engineering school and everything went swimmingly. Cari, the boss, was super cool—an American woman who had lived a solid chunk of her life in France already and built quite the empire along the way. She liked me enough for whatever reason and decided to take a risk on me despite my lack of teaching credentials (writing a few books and working as an English assistant earlier in life helped a lot—the fact

that she'd never seen me on camera and thus had low expectations for my looks probably didn't hurt either). I got the job. I felt relieved.

And then she said, "Great! Everything looks good to go from here. We'll have work for you in October."

October? It's April. I need to eat between now and then if I'm going to teach. Turns out the profit was a lie.

At least in the short term. My stress levels were rising to a screaming pitch. The school itself seemed nice and Cari was cool. I just needed something to tide me over. But I'd spent the last month navigating opening a business at the same time I'd been jumping through immigration hoops (imagine a similar level of dead-end futility but compounded by higher stakes and crueler bureaucrats). I was not in a good position, and English teaching was out of season. But I was a decent guide to my friends when they visited Paris. Maybe I could be a guide for money?

TIP AND I EAT

Back on that first trip to Paris, my parents and I had taken a tour with a little company called Bike About Tours. I think Christian was our guide, but it's a blur and I didn't take any photos. They sprang to mind immediately as an option, and my dad sent me a message around the same time with the same idea. "Why not be a bike guide?"

For one, it had been years since I'd biked anywhere. I've had enough motorcycle crashes to be leery of two-wheeled adventures in traffic.

For two. . .well. . .for two. . .I mean, why not?

I called up Bike About and a few other places—there was no more time for dillying nor dallying. I needed a job and I needed it now.

Fat Tire, Bike About's biggest competitor, got back to me first. They interviewed me and things seemed on the fast track to having a job. They were cool (Phil, if you're reading this, you're the only one who isn't cool—go take a shower); they just seemed so corporate—inflexible. Bike About, by contrast, took longer to get back to me but immediately offered me a job when I told them Fat Tire was knocking. The pay wasn't fixed to a salary but by tour. That made the hours flexible and opened up the opportunity for overtime as I needed.

I took the job.

Touring Paris on a bike is the best thing ever. OK, I'm overstating that because I want you to go book a tour with Bike About and make sure you give me credit, but it is definitely right at the top of the list of things to do in Paris.

Biking, for one, is a lot less work than walking. Within a few hours, we covered ground that would take all day to walk, from hidden portions of Philippe Auguste's wall to the Louvre, Place des Vosges to the Latin Quarter, and so many things in between.

Tourists, for two, are usually in very good moods. They're on vacation. They're in *Paris*. Getting paid to be the guy who knows his way around for a group of people who are excited just to be there is a combination for a good morning.

That isn't to say there weren't rough moments, like hungover kids off a Contiki tour ploughing straight into parked cars, or the random complaints from "That Guy" in the group through the entire tour. But it was overall a lot of fun.

It was an absolute treat to park my bike on a bridge over the Seine, point to any number of iconic landmarks around us, and tell jokes at the expense of our French hosts at large. Paris looks great when in motion around you, and after all the improvements to the roads and bike lanes, doing so by bike is pretty hard to beat (unless you've got a wheel, obviously, then you're on another level).

At this point, it should come as no surprise that I worked thirty days a month through the summer. I wasn't kidding when I said I needed money. As the season wore on, every euro I made got sent back to the States in the form of a debt payment. I had gotten to a place where I was paying $2,100 a month just to make my minimum payments. My rickety cracker barrel of a desperation ship was taking on water fast.

The first year of vlogging daily came to a close, fifty-four weeks in total, and I took a break. I had somewhere near 900 subscribers after a year of making videos every day. That's not even three subscribers per video. I loved doing it, but it felt like a failure and I needed a break.

I worked as much as I could, pulling two tours a day unless I was in Versailles, which is a full-day affair. I picked up more side jobs: web design, copywriting, and translation for CNRS (France's national scientific research division—Centre national de la recherche scientifique). I did everything I could to keep from going under, from losing this ship I'd finally used to escape sight of shore. The thing about losing sight of shore, of course, is that it makes sinking that much more lethal a problem.

I drank a lot that summer. I'd never been much of a drinker, but something about the constant risk of drowning combined with a never-ending work burden and the sudden release from my crushing production schedule might have had something to do with it. I don't think I picked up more than a solitary beer until my mid-twenties, living in the Congo. But hang out with a bunch of tour guides in peak season, especially the Irish ones, and you'll discover the depths of all sorts of new bottles. While I'm not proud of where things wound up that summer, I needed to blow off some steam. Thankfully, I exited with all fingers and toes accounted for.

Two other things happened that summer, two signs that I could no longer ignore.

The good one was that my YouTube channel, mysteriously, generously, had continued slowly growing even after I stopped making videos. This had never happened before, and I crossed the thousand-subscriber mark while on my break. It was the confirmation I needed that I was on to something. At least it was worth continuing. So, I geared up to make one more dive into the land of perpetual video life.

The second came shortly after, when the tours started slowing down and work was no longer so readily available. I was going to fall short and, for the first month ever, I was not going to be able to make my payments. Even if I gave these companies every penny, literally every cent I had, I would come up lacking. And they would begin to penalize me for it. I would find myself completely, humiliatingly broke, and I would also rapidly lose my credit rating, which was the only incentive to keep making those payments in the first place. The very definition of futility.

It was the slap in the face I needed. I needed to go bankrupt and I needed to do it now.

COWBOYS AND FIREFIGHTERS

I come from a line of manly men.

Grandpa Swanson contracted rheumatic fever at thirteen years of age, which left him bedridden for a year and permanently crippled. The doctors told him he'd never walk again, and for years, his friends would carry him up and down the stairs at school to help him get to class.

This, he found, was unacceptable. He learned to walk again. He learned to ski. And then he got his pilot's license. He wound up an agricultural professor at Washington State University.

Grandpa Lucas was the fire chief in Okanogan, Washington for nearly three decades. He was a mechanic, inventor, and a

fantastic storyteller. Where I never got to meet Grandpa Swanson (he died when my dad was a kid), my memories of Grandpa Lucas revolve around hunting, fishing, and fixing my car. He was a curmudgeon, to be sure, pipe hanging from his jaw or stuffed into his breast pocket at all hours, but his laugh lit up a room.

Between the cowboys, mechanics, firefighters, and farmers, you can see how I might have developed a bit of a work-ethic-as-personal-value complex. My dad isn't like this—he's a fantastic listener and the kind of guy who's not afraid to apologize when he screws up (probably the manliest trait of all). But there's plenty of room to get caught up in what a "real man" should be—whether or not it's ever explicitly said—and a "real man" pays his debts. No matter what.

If such a man falls on hard times, it's probably his own fault. He should have been smarter, even if we can agree he was unlucky. He should have known better.

It was very, very easy to see my own personal failings in the situation I'd created for myself. It was very difficult to see how perhaps this wasn't entirely my own fault and, even if it were, how there were legal and honorable ways of getting out. Bankruptcy is a tool, and one with its own set of consequences. I had avoided it for years, even as I was counseled to pursue it. I was scared it might jeopardize my ability to emigrate to France. Maybe it would threaten all of the intellectual property I had built up over the years.

I was terrified.

But as I sat in Le Peloton café in August of 2017, and I saw my bank account draining faster than it was filling, I knew I had to make a choice. It was a choice that made my face flush with itchy heat. My throat constricted as uncomfortably as I Googled bankruptcy lawyers and stepped outside to start making calls.

INTERNATIONAL MAN OF QUESTIONABLE DECISIONS

So, I learned a lot really quickly, but one of the things I realized over the process of returning to France was that the French not only don't care about American credit scores—they're pretty much unaware such scores exist. There would never have been any concern on their side as long as I could prove I was financially viable (which I wasn't), and no worries for me except I would have had to pay for everything in cash (which I THOUGHT I couldn't).

One of the first things the lawyer told me, once I found one willing to work with someone overseas at the time, was to stop paying everything. I was about to wreck my credit score anyway; it made no sense to pay my creditors for a few extra months. This not only felt immediately gratifying, if not guilt-inducing, but also served as a sudden revelation.

Between all of my hustles and side jobs, I was earning enough to live. For the first time in what might have been my entire life as an independent worker, I felt like I had actually built something. All of these side jobs, passion projects, all of it—I had built something that could support me. I simply never had the space to see it.

I had been terrified to fall behind without realizing I was already eating nothing but dust. Bankruptcy comes with its complications, logistically and socially, but it isn't wrong to ask for help.

That's not to say that going through the process wasn't still terrifying—it was—and it would require me to fly back to the States to sit in front of a real-life judge, prove my identity, and hope that my creditors didn't care enough to show up and claim my few possessions for themselves.

But here's the thing: I had unintentionally timed everything perfectly.

Here's a crash course in bankruptcy that you should not take any advice from because I'm not a lawyer. Bankruptcy, in America, is a form of protection from creditors when someone is in desperate need—it's meant to alleviate crushing debt and provide an opportunity to start over. So, in that spirit, there are certain floors under which creditors can't touch you.

If you have two cars, you're likely to lose one, but they can't take them both. Same goes for your house. They can take some of your stuff and sell it, but they can't take all of it. If you don't own anything or have any resources, they basically can't touch you at all.

Guess who didn't own anything or have any resources at the time but did have two thumbs? This guy.

The other pitfall of going bankrupt, especially when you're good and truly broke as a joke, is that it costs a few thousand dollars to do it. You can apply for it on your own for a fraction of the cost, but it's not advised to go without a lawyer. The odds of success on your own are slim to none, and skyrocket with legal help. So, all that money I was immediately saving on debt payments went straight into the legal fund instead. Fortunately, I was able to swing that for another few months. It was worth every penny.

If my debt was weighing down the ship, threatening to pull it under like a wayward anchor dragging through a reef, it was also counteracting the pull from weak financial winds. But those winds were changing, and I had been trimming my sails and streamlining the ship to compensate for all the deadweight and water leaking into my bilges. I had put a lot of work into this little desperation ship as we shuddered through the waves and out to sea together, and suddenly, I could see the results showing through. I couldn't have cut that anchor loose at a better time.

You Knew There Would be a Chapter on Patreon, Right?

That steady shift in the wind was thanks in large part to my Patrons.

I made a few commitments to myself as I entered my second season of vlogging daily, mostly centered on being more emotionally honest and vulnerable with my viewers. I hadn't let them in on my dashed hopes the previous year, weakening both the story and the connection with anyone watching. In order to change that, I had to be more open with what I wanted and where I hoped to go, no matter how hard or embarrassing that felt.

I also had to value my work as others valued it.

One of the lessons I learned in raising finances to volunteer with Mercy Ships had been to accept the generosity of others so they could participate in the work. Not everyone can pack up and move across the world, no matter how much they might want to—accepting their generosity in supporting the work was a very tangible way of including others in what Mercy Ships and I were up to.

It's a lot easier to reach out for financial help when the cause is as obvious as Mercy Ships'. It's much harder to see your own work in such a worthy light. But as is often the case, downplaying my work was as much a form of insecurity as it was a defense mechanism against the rejection of others. My videos were free, and would remain so, but there were people out there that wanted to see more of them. There were even people who were willing to put their money down to help me do so; I just needed to make it easier for them.

This is easier said than done when you're scared to put a monetary value to your own work. Thankfully, after a year of making a video every day with increasing levels of vulnerability, I

had stopped projecting my worst fears or impulses on the perceived opinions of others surrounding my work. Paid or not.

It turns out working really hard for very little galvanizes you over time—either to love what you're doing regardless, or to quit. I obviously wasn't quitting anytime soon.

I reformatted my Patreon, which was still geared towards my writing, and committed to promote it at least every other week and just see what happened. While it wasn't dramatic or immediate, there was always a steady uptick in support. Month by month it grew, until eventually, it was an income of its own.

There had been few experiences in my creative life up until that moment that were as transformative. Every notification that I gained a new Patron, and every exchange with them after, felt like the most tangible form of validation. These people didn't just like my videos or send me a comment to let me know it—they put their hard-earned cash down as proof that they wanted it to continue. They really believed in it. In me.

This slow, steady growth was timed perfectly because it was too small to amount to anything my creditors would care about but enough to move me in the right direction and start knocking out the need for certain side jobs. It felt very much like tossing loaded crates overboard right as the wind picked up and hit the sails at full force. The tar between the boards along my hull was sealing out the water, and the bilges were beginning to balance. And even though it would take another year to make up a full-time income, things began to accelerate very quickly. I was practically skimming across the surface of the water before I even realized we'd picked up speed.

CHAPTER TWELVE:
MAKING LANDFALL

FORTRESS OF THE DAMNED
(ON THE ISLE OF INSANITY)

THE WHIRLWIND

2017 and 2018 were close calls, navigating the bankruptcy process and working multiple jobs as I continued vlogging. If it weren't for the support of my parents, the generosity of my Grandlady, or the belief of my Patrons, I wouldn't have made it. As I write this, I'm still not 100% sure I'm going to.

We navigated the straits of financial woe, dodging shipwrecked opportunities and beached dreams along the way. The pull of the whirlpool grew weaker over time, along with the sense that any wrong turn would take me right back to it. And even if the winds slowed or shifted directions, they no longer faltered. My sails remained engaged.

I exited the hemisphere that had held me prisoner for years and entered a new one filled with promise and dangers of a different kind.

But since I know you really came here to hear more about life in France, let me toss you a couple of anecdotes about the joys and pains of life in Paris.

THE ISLAND OF INSANITY

As with any new adventure, there are gatekeepers along the way to moving to France. Especially if you want to stay. The immigration process is a maze in the least figurative sense possible. Answers are not forthcoming, especially when you don't know the actual title of the visa you're on. A two-headed monster, each head lying or telling the truth of its own accord depending on its disposition and the phase of the moon, would make for a more helpful bureaucratic interaction.

I had to visit three offices before being told definitively to go to a prefecture in northern Paris. This isn't a quick visit to three

offices near each other—this was three days of launching into the
ether to find one office, discern its riddles, discover the location
of my next quest, regroup, sleep, and try again the next day. The
final destination was not where I had assumed it would be, despite
going by the same name, a name you may even know a bit about
already: *prefecture*.

     This word is a slur. In many circles it's synonymous with
other words like *sadism*, *brimstone*, and *schadenfreude*. In reality, it's
a police headquarters, and for the immigration process, it's hell. I
can't imagine what criminals must go through, if my experience
is how they treat the law-abiding among us. Knowing France, it's
much more pleasant because of course it is.

     Previously, when I lived in France as an English assistant,
I was given instructions that laid out what documents I needed
to gather and where to deliver them from the get-go. This, I now
realize, was based entirely on the initiative of the teaching program
who, I'm sure, were sick of dealing with twenty-year-old assistants
on the verge of emotional meltdowns. Even with their help, it still
required a mind-bending run through what can best be described
as a physical exercise in circular logic.

     With this new, nameless visa, I had nothing but my previous
experience to guide me, which was how I eventually figured out
which prefecture to visit. What I couldn't figure out was how
much I was going to have to pay in taxes, nor when. I'd been told
"nothing," I didn't have to pay anything up front to process my
visa (which was a godsend for how little money I had on hand),
but I knew I would eventually have to pay *something*. Because of
course I would.

     Never trust anything that feels too good to be true,
especially when your immigration status is on the line.

     There was also the matter of figuring out literally everything
else I was supposed to do for this process. Upon arriving at the

northern prefecture, I discovered there was a line of people standing outside, which was set to take at least an hour and a half to get through. It formed down what could best be described as a narrow alley before snaking back towards the street. There were only ropes at the head of the line, so the rest of it was on an honor system. No one looked particularly happy with life. Less particularly happy than usual, I should clarify. The total lack of available seating made this misery manifest.

Seeing this bleak scene of human distress, and feeling a rumbly in my tumbly, I went and got lunch. I returned around 1 PM to find that the line had indeed moved, but I would have only moved a third of the way closer to its front. After another two hours of standing in the sun and wishing for a lawn chair, I managed to squeeze inside.

Imagine a small train station with a half dozen rows of short benches. Now imagine there's standing room only. That's what I walked into. I got to the counter and let them know why I was there, because of course there was no one to talk to outside, and they curtly let me know that I was missing a document no one had told me I needed. I had to come back the next day. *Because of course I did.*

This resulted in another couple of hours of waiting outside the next day, and waiting a few more inside, all to be told that the documents I brought weren't recent enough. This time, they told me to come back in a week and gave me an appointment, which graciously allowed me to skip the line. But by the time I finally got all of those documents together and handed in, I had only succeeded at passing through step number one.

After compiling my dossier, I was given an appointment at another prefecture altogether: the prefecture in the center of town.

THE PLACE THAT MAKES YOU MAD

There's an episode of the French cartoon *Astérix* dedicated to the idea of "the place that makes you mad"—it may be cloaked in Imperial Roman guise, but it is 100% inspired by French bureaucracy.

I won't get into the full insanity of it. You've gotten a taste. We'll move into a more picturesque vision of Paris in a moment.

But I will say that they ground me into a sticky pulp of quivering uncertainty. It would turn out much later that I had been sent to the wrong office, because no one knew what to do with me because, you guessed it, no one had ever heard of my visa before. Everyone involved was ignorant to this fact, however, for a very long time. And so, I wound up in the one dedicated to an immigration category the system subtly deemed "less desirable" and was treated in much the same way.

If you're struggling to read between the lines, this category is comprised of geographic/socioeconomic regions the French want to work extra hard to get into. There's a real tension in France that's different from the States in how they handle their former colonies (a sense of obligation) competing with the mindset that led to colonialism in the first place (basically racism).

For those who think the French don't struggle with race relations and identity politics: same foot, different shoe.

I digress. I sat in this cramped waiting area pinned between the door, one wall, and two lines of bank-teller desks in a long L. We were hemmed in, surrounded. Thoroughly cowed.

Wait for hours. You have an appointment for 9:30 AM. It doesn't matter; no one will see you until 1 PM at the earliest. I didn't get seen until 3 PM the first time. It turns out there's a tiny cafe in the central courtyard of that prefecture that sells snacks at discounts so low, they scrape the cobblestones. I did my shopping for the week while I waited.

When they finally called me up, I was subjected to more scrutiny than I could have expected.

"Why were you given this visa?" she demanded in an assault of French.

"Uh, because I asked for it?" There's no real way to answer a question like this—how am I supposed to know?

The lady to whom I was talking got up, walked over to talk to a colleague in a distant corner. Interrogation techniques: make the perp sweat. Fought to keep my cool.

She returned languidly, like there wasn't a room full of people waiting all day for their turn at the chopping block. "Why did they give it to you?"

"Because I applied?" Jeez, lady, cool it. "I'm an artist? It's an artist visa."

She leaned back, crossed her voluptuous arms, and stared me down. I shit thee not, she stared at me like I was a dried turd and she could light me on fire with pure disdain. This uncomfortable silence lasted for a few minutes before I cracked and started to state my case (which, I'll admit, was flimsy). This was summarily interrupted by her colleague, a man who until moments before I had thought of as a potential ally in this house of darkness.

He adjusted his glasses, put one hand down on my dossier, and leaned forward. "We don't think you deserve to be here."

Not an ally then. A statement like this will stun the breath right out of you. Thankfully, I had years of training for this— if nothing else, the years had taught me a little something of my worth. Or at least projecting some worth into a situation. I shrugged in deference, as if I too were uncertain of how I had managed it (which, to be fair, was true), then gestured back to the poor stack of paper under pressure and said, "Yet here I am."

The true power of the immigration system, as far as any power you may have, is knowing that these bureaucrats are stamps

at the end of a process they don't control. They are truly powerful, potentially lethal to one's future in France, but not without their limits. I already had the visa and, while I did need their final approval, had already successfully jumped through every hoop to get here.

That isn't to say I was a cool cucumber on the inside. My pulse was racing; I could have slid home on my palms. But in the moment, I sat there, a bored-yet-well-berated school child with nowhere better to go.

So, they gave me my three-month temporary stay and a handful of documents they wanted me to materialize out of thin air, and were done with me.

This is the second secret to success in the French immigration system: just stick with it.

They'll make you get "new" proof of residence every time, with fresh electricity bills as proof you haven't moved. They'll come up with outrageous documents and say you should have known to bring it when there was no way in the world you could have imagined it necessary. They'll run you around town, stare you down, glare at you, be downright rude, and you've just got to politely take it. Nod. Promise you'll do your best. Come back.

They get nicer with time. Normally. These jerks never did. I had to keep coming back every few months for a year for this treatment. Every appointment felt like drawing up a case before a very unfavorable judge, my life very much in the balance. It got so stressful, I saw an immigration lawyer for advice (which amounted to "Stay the course") and took multiple visits over an entire year before they finally realized, "You're supposed to be in the office upstairs." And with that, I was dismissed. Not their problem.

I was happy at the idea that I might never see them again.

The office upstairs also didn't know what to do with me; however, their response to this conundrum was to sit me down

with their department head. She combed through my entire dossier, which, by then, had gotten more substantial. She took the time to figure out what it was I was doing, how it all tied together, and how I was already making myself a productive member of Parisian society. She was genuinely kind.

Then she gave me the green light.

They took my fingerprints. Of course, I didn't realize that I was getting the green light in the moment—they still don't tell you anything. But I read the signs, held my breath, and two weeks later I got a text saying my "titre de séjour" was ready for pickup. It was pink, no larger than a driver's license, and I picked it up on February 28th, one day before my first anniversary in Paris.

Unlike the restraint I had shown in Vessel a year and ten days prior, that day, I danced out of there. That was the moment I also discovered my visa was good for another three years. I had suffered a long, stressful year, uncertain whether I was truly legal to work or allowed to stay. And in the end, I hit the jackpot.

THE ROOM TO CHATEAU

If you follow along with my vlog, you know about my tiny living quarters. If you're as-yet unaware, they're small. Thirteen square meters small (or 140 square feet, for the imperially minded). There's a shower and a sink and one small closet. If I shift my shirts too far to the right, I accidentally cut the electricity to the whole place. My toilet is at the end of the hall, because if you shoved it into my room, it would have to double as a desk chair.

I spent years sleeping on a mat in the corner. The furniture was designed for a French maid half my height and a quarter my size. The only desk was a sewing desk, sans machine, and to try and sit at it was to pinch off circulation to my legs at about seven different points. I had learned a lot, and one of those lessons was

to let in the generosity of others. My viewers saw the cramped and uncomfortable conditions—they heard me pine for a warmer existence and saw my designs for a more efficient use of the space. They came through in a big way.

Suddenly I was sleeping in my Cozy Cloud™ six and a half feet off the ground. It was thanks to the generosity of my Grandlady that the mezzanine bed happened. It was thanks to my Patrons and fans at large that the place got thoroughly transformed.

This transformation mirrored the one that took place in my life: from struggling in discomfort and near-poverty just to make ends meet, to suddenly having a place I could not only call my own but in which I felt comfortable and happy.

A lot of my drive to explore the city was generated by a sense of cabin fever. I struck out into Paris as much to guard my sanity as anything else. Now returning home added stability and solved for sanity. I love my CozyCloud™ and comfy chateau.

Paris itself is home in a new way as well. When I first got back to the city, I made it a mission to know it better than I ever had and to share that exploration with the world. In pulling off the gas, I realized just how comfortable I had come to feel in the capital.

Whether it's along the bustling thoroughfare sandwiching Canal Saint-Martin, the bike lanes along the banks of the Seine, or the rustling paths crisscrossing the Jardin du Luxembourg—I always have friends a stone's throw away.

This happened quietly in the background as I vlogged my way around town, nose to the grindstone, translating scripts and teaching courses on how to run a Kickstarter. What a pleasant surprise to find, as I slowed down and lifted my head to look around, that I was surrounded by smiling faces.

And how invaluable now, as I write this, in a strange period of redefinition and rediscovery.

THE SEA OF THE UNKNOWN

The sun breaks over the horizon, jutting towards us in red bursts between cresting waves below and the remnants of last night's storm above. The pull of the tide is fully behind us now, even the threat of the whirlpool a fast-fading fear. The sirens and krakens aren't all behind us, either; that much has been made clear in the years we've been at sea. There are always more monsters, dangers unknown lurking behind any distant wave.

But we made it past them. We survived, learned from the close calls, and did better at dodging the next.

The sails snap overhead, pulled by a fresh gale off the volcanic island behind us. There's no time to dwell on what small scraps of land we've found so far. They're comfortable, calm after the raging storms and sleepless nights at their mercy. They offer a blessed respite, wonderful moments where we can breathe without fear of sinking, but they're not our destination.

That remains out on the open sea, beyond the horizon in a place that only our souls know of and our hopes hold in an ever-tightening grasp. The voyage has only just begun, which is exciting for its promise and slightly depressing for how long we've already been at sea. Considering the struggle just to get here, it sometimes feels like a lifetime or two have already passed in pursuit of something that may have never existed in the first place.

The sun pulls itself above the horizon, erupting in the golden light of our futures before steadily dimming in the clouds. The wind swirls around the decks in response, crisp and fresh. These moments used to make us shiver and wrap up against the oncoming challenge of the day. But now it sparks a relish for the voyage.

No one said it would be easy, or even possible. In fact, most of them said precisely the opposite. We aren't out here with

the cold spray in our faces and salt in our eyes because it's pleasant. We don't row when the wind dies, pull splinters from between our fingers, and patch sails because it's leisurely. We do so because we're called to it.

We sail because, truly, we have no other choice.

Whether we find the beacon that calls to our hearts, whether it quells our thirst and calms our souls when we reach it, or whether we die in the effort without ever catching sight of its shores, we do so willingly. We do so joyfully. Because we suffer all these things in the hopes that we are something more. A part of something greater than ourselves. It only took a few near-drownings to sharpen us to the calling. To harden us against its demand for sacrifice.

Besides, we all die one way or another. Better to do so in pursuit of something we love than sitting on the Shores of the Known, wishing we'd cast off when we were still thirsty and able-bodied.

EPILOGUE OF THE UNKNOWN

There were a lot of metaphors that captured the feel of the last decade. I could have leaned into any of them, but the Sea of the Unknown seemed the most poignant and best tied into multiple elements of my life. The one that my dad and I often talked about, while ambling around the Inland Northwest, was the ditch through which I found myself crawling. At least I hoped I was crawling through it—there were times that it really felt like I might have been slinking endlessly along its bottom.

No matter how hard I tried, I couldn't seem to find a way up and over the edge. I wasn't sure there was an edge, and for a long time I couldn't even see changes in the light that might indicate I was making any progress. This book is meant for anyone who has ever found themselves in a similar place. Your story may look different, be somehow more or less dramatic, but it's yours and it's valid in its own ways. I hope you never give up hope.

In revisiting the last decade I've hit on a couple of things that were helpful to see on the page, but none so much as the act of taking on the perspective of an interlocutor. Vlogging daily

had a similar effect. One helpful thing to observe in writing this was the cycles into which I constantly fell, but also seeing how many appear to be coming to their close. The ways in which I approached relationships, money, work, and self-valuation showed up in patterns that only really began to break for good in the last few years. Some of those cycles shattered at the apex of crisis, like stepping out of the Peloton Café in the summer of 2017, calling lawyers in the US from Rue du Pont Louis-Philippe under the realization that I needed to start over financially. I've lived 100% debt-free ever since.

Others continued crumbling until I stared them in the face through the process of writing all this out. They cracked as I came to love myself as reflected through these stories, despite the struggles sparked by my shortcomings and stupidity.

This was precluded by vlogging daily though, much like an audio/visual practice run. I learned to listen to myself and reframe my thoughts to align with how I wanted to consider my circumstances, redoing my garage monologues until I discovered a path I wanted to take forward, one that was simultaneously honest and optimistic. In many ways, this book is an extension of those monologues. Writing out an entire book on the adventures that led me to Paris, giving myself time—listening to myself—was a key step in learning to accept myself for who I am. Changing my perspective through narrating my life helped me step to the side and see it from a different angle, one in which I found less shame and more empathy for the battered man stumbling headlong towards his impossible dreams.

Being accepted by a small audience along the way lifted a good portion of the burden as well. Throwing myself into subjects that terrified me only to be caught by a plethora of digital hands taught me a lot—not least of all about how I was truly my own harshest critic. Thank you for being a part of the process.

About the conclusion of this book, I found a way out of the ditch. I saw the light shifting as I got my visa to France, and even though the path up and over the edge was fraught with dangers of its own, I managed to shuffle over them and get out. I didn't feel like I'd exited for a long time, I always felt like I was at risk of getting dragged right back down to the bottom, but over the course of the next two years I stopped being afraid. I looked around at my cozy chateau, the fact that I could hire an assistant, and started to feel like maybe—just maybe—I was going to make it out of this alive. Possibly even in decent shape.

Of course as things finally picked up in Paris, I also came to a crashing halt of a different variety. One cycle I have yet to fully break is working myself overhard until I burn out. Vlogging daily put me in another deep hole, paradoxically giving me a shot at a life I'd always wanted in the midst of removing my ability to carry on with it (or fully appreciate what I had). But if I stop and look around, like I've had the good fortune to do here, I'm amazed at how far out into the Sea of the Unknown I've been able to make it. So far, in fact, that I'm comfortable and confident in making this archipelago into which I've stumbled my new base of operations.

Even as we lock down in Paris for COVID-19, I feel like the winds are picking up again. This time I have a decent ship with fully-trimmed sails, ready to capture that wind more fully than ever before. We don't know what will come next, but we can be certain that challenges and hardship will always be somewhere over the horizon. It's not a matter of if, but when, and then as now as always before: it's a matter of putting our hands to the work of sailing through the storm to find whatever lies beyond.

My voyage is far from over. The Sea of the Unknown lies open before me. And I will heed the call of that distant beacon, be it destiny or doom, 'til I reach its shores or succumb to whatever fate gets the best of me. I hope you'll join me.

ACKNOWLEDGEMENTS

This book wouldn't have been possible without you (yes, you), first and foremost. Whether you're a longtime fan of my vlog or a longer-time fan of my fiction, just being here has made more difference than you know. If you're a Patron of mine, or ever were at any point, I hope that you understand better now than ever just how vital you were to keeping my head above water.

For my dad—for providing where you could, in the ways you could, and always being there to listen. Kaarin for always being a supportive and helping hand, Kevin for helping despite your skepticism ;P and Grandma Jane for watching my vlog every day despite the technical challenges involved. And thanks, Mom, for getting me out and into the world despite my oversized head.

Jefe, Nolan, and Slush—the ever-supporters of my work regardless of genre. Natasha for her endless, radiant joy. My Patrons for making such a massive difference—you're *all* included in a few pages—especially Susan, Jani, Dixie, Mystery Man, Rob, David, and Maxime for your wildly generous contributions both to the chateau and beyond, as well as your constant enthusiasm –

even Dave for your bloody obsessions, and Eric for 'Delta' reading this book as we put the finishing touches on it. And of course thank you to everyone who backed this book on Kickstarter in the first place!

Thanks to Kate for helping keep my aforementioned Patrons happy campers, and keeping me sane in the process. And a massive thank you is due to my ultimate, classiest Patron and Grandlady, Kiki. If it wasn't for you, I wouldn't have been able to move back to Paris and make this a fresh start in the first place.

Of course, above all, thanks to Richard whose notes and guidance made this book about ten times better than it otherwise would have been. You're a great friend, with or without Gustave nipping at your heels, and a good man in general whose sense of empathy and compassion for the world around you continues to inspire.

I tried to toss credit where it was due throughout the book but, as I'm sure you might guess, I could continue thanking people until I ran out of pages and far beyond. We can save those stories for another book (let me know if you'd like more of these). Thank you so much, unnamed heroes; if I failed to give you credit here, I can always buy you an appreciative apology beer as soon as we're out of quarantine.

There's so much more to come—this really is only the beginning.

If you've struggled with anything I mentioned in this book, especially depression or any form of mental illness, please don't hesitate to reach out to someone in your local community for help. Whether it's your mental or emotional health, financial struggles, or straight-up loneliness—sitting there by yourself isn't going to get you any closer to putting this chapter behind you. Believe me, life is better lived with friends and there's no shame in asking for help from the people around you.

I hope you enjoyed this voyage into the *Sea of the Unknown*! Share it with someone you know will enjoy it, too. Until then, I'll see you bright and early some Monday morning soon over on YouTube.

And again, to my Patrons, all of whom pitched in to varying degrees for differing amounts of time over the last few years. You changed my life. More than that, you made a happy ending to this book possible. Thank you a million times over <3

Here's everyone who's ever given me so much as a single dollar on Patreon, listed by the order in which they first pledged, in the exact way they entered it on the site. Can you believe over half of them are still with me today? That's nuts!

Joel Pearson
Nimit Malavia
Joe Longworth
Keleren
Wayne Fang
Xeribo
Brian Anderson
Matt Rogers
Erin Collective
Jeff Beltran
Erik Rammelsberg
David Patierno
Adam Rakunas
Kevin Crain
Nolan Stamm
Amy
Jennica Vincent
Megan Slankard
Cassie Fairfield
Dave Robison
Kaarin Howard
Dylhan Lievin
François Robin
Eduardo Hernández-Pacheco Acosta
Steve Weaver
Allison Richter
Anna Tinsman
Jeremiah Reinmiller
DFTBAndy

Tim Morgan
Theo Schwebel
annee
Patrick Welch
Ali Herbert
Cynthia Shepherd
Pierre Lacave
E
Larry Vargas
Ethan Gates
Joshua Pimental
Nicole Johnson
Nicole Taylor
Grace Seow
Desiree Logue Champagne
Dennis Gonzales
Amber
Blake Travis
Carla Measer-Costamagna
Maxime
Jon Beatty
Joseph S.D. Cross II
Jürgen Finger
Ariana Forby
Mykolas Tikuišis
Rebecca Arntson
Steven Hoglund
K Nguyen

Chuck Jordan
Kieran Hegarty
Ashley Guerrero
Quellessi
Jorge Rivera
Carlo Lombardo
Daniel King
Andres Aguirre
Ann S
Shalee Gold
Abdelamir Darwiche
Neville Llewellyn
Marion Fregeac
AsylumHDGaming
Cynthie Thomas
NormaJ
Alexander James Howe
Kim Do
Lawrence Garcia
Shuray Merriweather
Tim Brush
Max Petch
Dawn Boquist
Kit Kan
Marisol
angelofthenorf
Zoey Arielle
Stephanie Bundle
Cheryl NonStopParis
Brie

Rachel Gibbs
jelitsa legarreta
Linda Adams
Sonja Bajic
Nils Swanson
Linara Siqueira
Jade Elliott
Jennie Campos
Matt
Joshua Young
stewart bergevin
K. C. Alexander
Megan Shelton
Nathan Slabaugh
David Meyer
Shannon Woody
Courtney Taylor
Julie
heidi williams
Wolf Weintraub
Alli Rowedder
Kim Clark
Ashley Collins
Elaine Vincent
Morgane Hervé
Patrick Cecil
Craig Hughes
Debi Lockhart
Katja Beer
Salv
Clayton Hadiken-Hyra
Anna Johnston
Antonietta Carpanzano
Tiffany Striga
Maria Smith
Joel Aiken
Amy Gruber
Chloe Clark
Lindsey Watts
moreau thierry
Elizabeth Rios
Liz James
Steve Stark
Kathryn Barnes
Ivanov Sasha
Rodrigo Acuna
Vicki Lappin
Jason Jones
ToreeDoesThings
Mathilde

Emelie Pauli
Cheryl Stephenson
Andrew Pandis
Anonymous
Stephen Wilson
Emily Yang
Rachel Muircroft
Trevor Jones
Dixie Rose
Tim Lingel
Teresa Hurtado
Toby Lewellen
Kelly Durgan
Jasmin Jackson
Claudine Hemingway
Howard Taft
Dale A Richards
Rahul Kumar
Laine Johnson
Shelah Miner
Kevin Van Lohuizen
Krista D. Ball
Jonathan Palo
Tal kalontarov
ginger solis
Shelley Price
Greg M
Juliette Morris Williams
John Polanszky
Robert Colburn
Suzanne Butler
Jani Hukkanen
Anita Shetter Johnson
Debbie Merced
Sarah Anoke
Renee
Farah Asif
Alex Dorcy
Lavender He
William Inglis
WakeboardBot
Ariadna
Kevin P Willard
Lou Daprile
Cameron Bardas
Kevin Mcleod
John Springate
Don & Whitney Lafond
Noël Soisson
Laurie Witham

Tracey Kinney
Pedro X Garcia
Kristoffer Karlsson
Catherine Pryor
Cammie Archuleta
Sonia Nava
Amy Hooper
Karley Violet
judi miehl
Sheri Willard
Muriel
David Romero
Kevin Croswhite
Kelley Lynne Riggs
trace
Rachel White
Jodi Marie Mackin
Andrea Almassy
Dee Griffin
Mike Trebert
Jennifer Gross
Nancy Prosser
Niva Canedo
Karen Giron
Greg Williams
Bonnie Eason
Carmen Pagnotta
ChantalTV
Patricia Hallam
Andrea Rennia & Marco Rennia
Rachel Ropp
Edgardo Cordero
David R. Hendrickson
Nicole Partington
Nanette Davis
Rich Parry
Margo A C
Elena Delavega
Addie Graham
Thomas Semrok
Maria Kristina Melgarejo
Brad
Nate
Heather Cutting
Gerald Lee
Andrea Soyer
Jana Miranda
Elizabeth Ruesch

D'Juana Conner
Lillian Brazin
Jose Arroyo
Saundra Hendricks
Chris Bates
Patrina McBride
Nancy Huhta
Kirsten Boys
Micah C
Jeremy Frank
Mike Fye
Jeff & Colleen
Nikki wyte
Brian Glenn Proulx
Peter Goelen
Grace Gonzalez
SK
Sparrow Butler
Enrique Gutierrez
John Buchan
Anna Adora
Sean Ector
Molly E Ayre-Svingen
Palm Trees In Paris
Susan French
Duane Touchet
Emily Goodin
Dr. Jamie Johnson
Cecillia Berger
Rita Gordon
Jonah Barla
Chris Vaughn
Kristen Gilbert
Tracy Lacue
Terria Velez
Paige Anderson
Ellen Goldstein
Chloe Elliott
Jill Holzapfel
Teresa Bunting
Mira Verma
Aaron, Teresa and Larry Blair
Kathleen Maria Bechtol
Dylan Mohr
Peter Hocking
Seana
Kerrin-gai Hofst-rand-easom
Nicholas Aspinwall

Zach Egan
Kerry James
Christelle
darren lucas
Jose Nanin
Kiya W
Gary Theosophilus
Kelly Tungland
John Tedorski
Dontrell Thomas
Steven Bullock
Ashley Shumard
Ben Kempf
Valerie Hannan
Jeremiah Ruesch
Shaikha Balqis
Raquel Costelli
Stephen Meier
Marilyn Lopez
Eric Leszkowicz
Danya S.
Elizabeth Reagan
Barbara Bidot
Janine Davey
Jenn Castano
Rob Christian
Lucy Bonomo
Tuan Thai
Nick Moys
Jeff White
Erin Bridges
Bryan Wells
Shemicka Simpson
Jesse Gearhart
Mark Williams
Eric Stevens
Gafner
Chris Findley
The Wandering Gene-alogist
Paige Harms
Richard Walters
Jeffery L Powell
Shauna Lee
Katherine Weber
M.Chap
Barbara Livieri
Grady Bolton
Joseph Fisher
Sandra P Caubel

Fred Wells
Wendy Cox
David Guy
Jacky L Loehr
Martin Hawley
Jennifer
Alicia Hutchinson
Joe Tromsness
Ashley
Nestor Lopez
Carol Leung
Chris Gaines
Roger
KATE NEUFELD
David William Cooke
LeeAnna Adkins Online
Dorothy Richardson
Ilya
Katie Van Wyngarden
Susan Davenport
Daryl Winchester
Jennifer Erickson
Jordan Fox
Jessica Ryugo
Jennifer Briasco
LORELEI HOLLY
Danielle Wallis
Justin Grizard
NancyJ
Ronda Lawson
Mary
Megan Heeke
Gary Williams
Michele Sibert
anne kowalsky
Angelyn Burk
Neil Littler
Paul HORTON
Kenyatta Gatlin
Fanni Huttunen
Steve Oswald
David Novy
Gini Wallace
Eddie Carey
Al Cain
Tara Cordova
Maura Fertich
Ashley Massey
Beth Hughes
Mary Di Giorgio

Judith Conrad
Colby Brunson
Jose Padron
Axel Yezeguelian
Teresa Poole
Lana McLaurin
William Ghozali
Pam Smith
Jennifer Seale Connell
Amy Marie
Hiker In Estonia
Yonatan Miller
Mike Riddles
Steven Sorensen
Virginie
Richard Filippetti
Scott Bradley
Kim Byer
Heather Pickett
Eric Norris
Jane Baker
Vickie D'Aversa
Lori Henry
Joe Borsuk, Artist
Karla and Laura
Ann Guin
Roj4ck
Paige Crosswhite
Kerry Bartlett
Jennifer Valente
Iain Sutherland
Jani Thacker
Hilaryn Tolosa
Scott Lovell
Matt Thompson
Shelley Fuller
Cat
Sean Price
Kelly Pires
Linda Mahiram Raphael
Amanda
Shelly Dyer
Dorothy Kelly
Charlie Sparrow
Cecily Widmann
Marjolein Mantel
Gonzalo Middleton
Barend Koorts
Anthony Buonincontri
Cindy M Hartigan

Scott Crawford
Kym Motley
Cindy Zackney
Scott Kennedy
Natalie Sullaway
Cori Wilbur
Amanda Sargent
Rona BerryMorin
Bron X
Socorro
nicholas wray
Sheryl Ann Fiore
Amy Schiavo
Amy Rothermel
Bill
Stephen Wood
William Hart
Carter Blumeyer
Sebastien Lessard
Jeffrey Edgar
Ernie Wellman
David C Adams
Crowfoot
Amanda McAllister
Patricia FLESHMAN
Joseph Brouillard
Kelly D. Crowe
Jenni Schweitzer
Zach
Max Prentl
Matt Lowe
Jim Garrison
Mitch Barney
Kat Butler
Michael
Glenn Camp
Thomas Baity
Erica Ramey
Gina Funmaker
Kathleen Hobbs
Luca Schumann
Florentina Bettendorf
Sam P
Danielle Simpson
Linda Elizabeth Ballan-
tyne
Rachel Ambrose
Crystal
Founder Timless Capital
Mike Place

Steven
Adi Ben-Yehuda
Jafe Campbell
Adrianne Byrd
Vanessa Aviles
Pamela Seno Magbiray
Rebecca Torres
Aloraluna
Tekela Tarvin
Cynthia Stewart
William King
Eileen Babbitt
Stephanie DRURY
Louie
Alexandra Bethard
Mr & Mrs. DJ Poseur
Martin Ocando
Josh Garrett
Brad Wiedrich
Aaron Leavelle
Frédéric Marcellin
Carl Garbie-Rivera
Stark Suicide
Madison LeBlanc
Cassie Cagwin
Jozilyn Muniz
mike culkin
Joshua Pulsifer
Trevor Valdez
Chris Smith
Raul Enciso
Bobby Ying
Anastasia
Erin Jean Backman
Taylor
Seth Crosland
Beth Murphy
Ryan Grass
William LaRue
Michael Connor
Ami Beattie Johnson
Pineapple Betty
Julia Hews-Everettt
Jacob Harris
David Hicks
Mike Morlan
Ken Edwards
matt malo
Jennifer Bruce-Dorsett
Amy

Eric Scott
Steve Leis
Gina Penn
Debra Coulter
Rachel Gibbs
Rhea S
Nick Clarke
Kendra Lawyer
Sheryl Sandige
Adam Thompson
Chris Tio
Paul Greenlee
Amy
David Carns
Dan Bonser
Minh Son
Christopher Morton
Bobby
Gladys Hernandez
-Tufegdzich
Alan
Marco Lozada
Katy
Michael Terry
Jared Baxter
Lara Martini
AMY M TERZINO
Ana
Kyle O'Guin
Deb Guillot-Fife
Roger La France
Johana Castro
RL Red
Sonny Greenwich Jr
Teresa Peterson
Constanza Browning
Nancy Jarnecke
Justin Foster
Lida Randolph
Tami Brown Blatecky
Joseph Hoh
Carolyn Fromm
Patrick McBride
Michael Monn
Kat
Vicki Sheerin
CHARLES DECKER
Gabrielle Corbett
Sam Mangham
Christine Schmidutz

Hugh Williamson
Emma Ashing
Kelly Meredith
Jacqueline Pye
Curtis Cooper
Sandra Veneklaas
Nancy
Erin Houlihan
Rod Tussing
Melissa Webb
Ray Waliany
B MANGO
Anne Sandstrom
Sonia
roberta
Joseph Banks
Jay McGary
Ashley Knudson
Naiomi Washington
Amanda Ramsay
Ray Minton
Shawn Dempsey
Cara
Joe Watson
Michael Raillard
Marie Hornung
Judith DeLong
Mike Haas
Elizabeth Olivier
Stephanie Grein
Swiss
Hwaida Sweilem
Leah Tatum
Annie-Michelle Arse-
neault
Martha Cuevas
Michael Grant
Marnie Wilson
PAUL MACK
lawrence mclennan
Mark Leidich
Eric Birkett
Filipe Nunes
Brandon Schellhase
Danielle, IBCLC
Megan Tucker
Geri Cheng
Jillanne Kukulis
Jacquelyn Anne
Sarah Black

Alicia Toombs
adhocs
Katherine
Braxton Duke
Mark Vicars
Trudy Farrar
Steve Kurtz
Rachel Foss
Maria Rodi
Honey Lynn
Brian
Xuan Nguyen
Ali Rodriguez
Lyndsey Connal
Jeff Thompson
DRob
Catherine Rochell
James Burgess
Michelle
Mashedmelissa
Jason Saphara
MattwithTwoTees
Tiffanie Randall
Blair
Alty Wilson
William McLeod
Ginette
Stephen Eckert
Linda Ciaravino
Captain Roger Victor
Christi Donati
Barbara Jones
Judy Makowski
Jenae Esquibel
Sasha Perkins
Brianna Lamberson
Bill L'Herault
Al Sweeney
Christine Gamble
Author Bert Edens
Suzanne Moore
Todd Gillette
Cheryl Greene
Jon
Laura Mae Galbraith
Jenny PalmTree
Chris Hatfield
Jane Jensen
Sue Ann
Owen Stephens

Melissa Shumake
Jeff Ward
Justin Estevanell
Max Shenk
Amy Kleinbach
Mark and Roberta Peterson
Alejandro Lopez
gary vaught vaught
David Cross
Cornelia
Michelle Martin
Brian Rain
Steven Hunt
Kim Myers
Lisa Hammer
Nola Garegnani
Zuzana
Ken Marquez
Christopher Kelsey
shannon dettrow
Ian Mcnulty
Shelley Qiu
Jorge R Callejas
russell king
Kathy Beezley
Jain Thorne
Karen Lee
Jennifer Lincourt
Jasmin
Jo-ann Oaks
Frankie and Clifton
LISA L MORTER
Monique Choiniere
Brad
Jeff Blackburn
Julie McKee
ACZero
Andrea
Emily Brooks
Linda M Mills
Suanne Ali
Karin Bates
Lucinda Murphy
Leighton Smith
B
Kim Johnson
John Murray
D Crenshaw
Wyat Kvalvik

Diana Theriault
Tracie Root
Margaret McManus
Robert Krieg
Scott D'Errico
Victor Charpentier
Billy Hawkins
Danielle Violot
Jakk Scarlett
Jennifer Ceci
Richard Mortenson
Jemma Fisk
John Maryn
Jennifer Olson
Bryn Jones
Karey
Rachel Wright
Christopher Berinato
Kurt Prindiville
Amelita B Hill
Yiskah Tucker
Kathryn
Mats Rosenqvist
Michael Dunham
Tim & Ashley
Carrie Roth
Suzanne Valentine
Marko
April Galash
Steve Guberman
Kathie Chetty
Joe Steinbring
Joe Lawrence
Mark Lesher
Robyne Stewart
Bryant Dunbar
Toni Santos
Stephanie Sanchez
jillian b
Stacee Kersley
Paul Canavan
Toni M Bryant
Gerri Matthews
SMary Demner
gidget nazareno
Leann Ling
David carlock
kris unkel-palchick
Mallory Corkins
Brian Fitzgerald The

Golf Doctor
Gabrielle
Jen Mendoza
Aaron D Hill
Andrew Kenning
John Hedderman
Marvin Colon
Juanito
Amela Cenanovic
Kevin
Peggy
SMary Demner
Maria Trenzado
Rich Valenta
Debra Lesser
Kathie Leno
Elljoworld
Eric Landaverry
Lucy Sansom
Jo-anne m
David
Cletus Bower
Evan Delay
Wendy Alexander
Nick Terranova
Nathaniel Drew
Dread Gods
Judy Longcore
Dennis Valk
Michael
Linda Droege
Dean Thompson
Mark Cassle
Greg and Kathy Jennings
Debbie Hogshead
Danny O'Brien
Sheri Ashton
John Rizzo
J Mac
Jynefer Watson
Paul Delong
Cole Vanden Heuvel
Oliver Gee
Lynn Pearson
Strongtree Coffee Roasters
Monique Krainz
Peter Stangert
Tucker S
Heather Hilton

Steve
Matt Killen
Todd Strehlke
Jody Ferguson
Steve Drew
Jorgen Bernle
Liz Bradshaw
Chudney Thomas
Hillary Franklin
Carmen L
Hayden Gullins
Hilary Peace
figures.seven.three
Katy Stephens
Kathyrn Ross
Aaron Figueroa
Allison Timmins
Judith K Longcore
Lost With Littles

Jodie & Paul Bourke
Andy Nelson
Jacquie Slater
Heidi Boyd
Holly Elissa
Patricia A C
Susan Treanor
Cody
Shelly Campbell
Juneli Dungca
Todd Johnson
James Cameron
Monica
Craig Cameron
Tone
Alex Marc
Anthony Casselman
Troy Bowman
Deborah Lanteigne

Thank you all so very much – you changed my life and enabled the creation of this book (among so many other things).

ABOUT THE AUTHOR

Seriously? You haven't had enough of this yet?

How about where to find me if you don't already know: I'm still making videos on YouTube regularly (though not daily anymore) and you can find them by searching for my name (you'll find that at the top of half of the pages in this book if you forgot already). Same with my photo/day project which is ongoing, and can be found on Instagram under the same name (hint: it's surprisingly close to 'Ron Swanson').

I still live in Paris and, as I write this, am currently under lockdown with my agave plant, Gilly. She's doing fine, thanks for asking.

If you enjoyed this book, please give it a review on Amazon or Goodreads and then share it with someone you think would benefit from reading about my mistakes. If you'd like to track with my publishing ambitions, my editor, Richard and I produce a podcast about it: *Building the Oracle*. Give it a listen!

Stay safe out there, and wash your hands!

Thanks for reading! Follow me on:
Instagram @jayswanson
Twitter @jayonaboat

My podcast can be found at www.buildingtheoracle.com or by searching for "Building the Oracle" wherever you listen to your favorite podcasts.

And subscribe to my newsletter for regular insights into life in Paris, photos, recipes, and sneak peeks at things like this book: www.jayswanson.me/newsletter

jayswanson
Musée du Louvre

Liked by **kaarins** and **1,136 others**

yswanson 1 photo/day 3,379: goodnight Paris; our oughts are with the rest of the world as we head t... more

ew all 30 comments

www.ingramcontent.com/pod-product-compliance
Lightning Source LLC
Chambersburg PA
CBHW070029100426
42740CB00013B/2633